UND
ERL
INE

UEA Undergraduate
Creative Writing Anthology
2018

UNDERLINE

*UEA Undergraduate
Creative Writing Anthology
2018*

Underline

A NOTE FROM THE EDTIORS

Here we are, turning the pages of yet another finished Undergraduate Creative Writing Anthology which, on its fifth edition, continues to pay tribute to the love that students have of literature and their ambition to set foot in the publishing industry. Taking the legacy of last year's project, which was written, edited and published by students, *Underline* symbolises our commitment to deliver the best possible collection of writing that UEA's undergraduates can produce.

This Anthology is Egg Box's main project, and one of the most important ones many of us have ever been involved with. We are not only a publisher, but a student-led society that promotes our love of publishing amongst all students regardless of their degree. We offer opportunities to get involved in collaborative projects such as the editing of the object you hold in your hands, where dozens of rigorous students-turned-editors carefully read, selected and appreciated every word that well over one hundred students sent for us to consider. As a community of writers and editors, students have engaged with each other's work to craft the final version of *Underline*, an anthology that acts as a celebration of literature's triumph amongst UEA's body of students.

We are undergraduates, with career paths yet to be set and lives yet to discover. What the prefix 'under' adds is a mysterious and hidden aspect to the words to which it is attached. But as opposed to previous years, we wanted to choose a uniquely celebratory title that highlights the strength of our collaborative publication, where students voluntarily take part in crafting the project that represents the undergraduate work of one of the most prominent departments of Creative Writing in the country. *Underline* pays tribute to the common effort that students, collaborating with staff, have made to create it.

Without the indispensable initiative and support of Nathan Hamilton and Philip Langeskov, as well as the funding of the school of Literature, Drama and Creative Writing, this project would not have been possible, and with it the invaluable experience that we, as students, will benefit from while embarking into the professional world. As the Anthology editorial team, we hope you feel the rigour and the care with which we have handled every detail and every sentence of this publication, and enjoy students' stories, reflections and powerful writing as much as we have.

The *Underline* Team

CONTENTS

NEVERSINK *Claudia Besant*	1
'YUGTO' *Amy Bonar*	5
RESTART FROM LAST CHECKPOINT? *Daniel Box*	14
COME HOME JETHRO *Martha Boyd*	16
BOYS *Felicity Brown*	19
A FIFTY PERCENT CHANCE OF A FUTURE *Sophie Bunce*	23
SHE AND HER *Chloe Crowther*	26
TIGER TIGER *Grace Curtis*	30
SKIN OFF YOUR LIPS *Ella Dorman-Gajic*	35
NO DICE *Basil Eagle*	37
THE PROCESS OF DYING *Gus Edgar*	42
TO PAINT WITH THE BLOOD OF OTHERS *Sam Edwards*	45
TREASURE HUNT *Abbey Hancock*	48
ONE REBELLIOUS STRAND *Zaid Hassan*	52
FOR THOSE WHO'VE COME *Liam Heitmann-Rice*	56
PROXIMITY *Judith Howe*	61
BETWEEN THE LINES *Becca Joyce*	62
WINTER'S FOR FIDELITY *Mari Lavelle-Hill*	67
CHIAROSCURO *Mari Lavelle-Hill*	68
THE WORLD ACCORDING TO K *Shannon Elizabeth Lewis*	69
KITCHEN SCENES *Jaime Lock*	72
RING *Jaime Lock*	73
ON GASSING PIGS *Jaime Lock*	74
WHEN SHALL WE HEAR FROM LOBSTER? (OR THE STORY OF THE FASCINATING MAN) *Adam Maric-Cleaver*	75
GADD. *Lucy May*	80
STAINLESS *Lucy May*	81
WEDNESDAY'S CHILD *Lucy May*	82
WAITING FOR THE NEXT BUS AT THE CORNER OF OLD RD *Jono McDermott*	83
COLLECTION OF POETRY BY ELLIE MEIKLE *Ellie Meikle*	87
THE FOURTH WALL *Catherine Mellor*	89
PASTEL COLOURED WINTER *Magdalena Meza Mitcher*	94

RED LION / BLACK DOG *Tamar Moshkovitz*	98
THE FELTON GREEN COUNTY WOMEN'S SOCIAL CLUB *Eilish Mullane*	100
THE WALL IN THE WAVES *Matthew Nixon*	105
AT FIRST SIGHT *Alyssa Ollivier-Tabukashvili*	107
SO FAR SO GOOD *Henry Opina*	113
BLEED *Henry Opina*	114
NAME *Cara Ow*	115
SHOWERS *Georgina Pearsall*	116
THE BAD BATCH. *Johnny Raspin*	120
ASTRAEA *Ellie Reeves*	124
FORTY DAYS AND FORTY NIGHTS *Ellie Reeves*	125
WRITTEN WITH A RENTED HAND *Ellie Reeves*	126
INDEPENDENCE DATE *Fiona Sangster*	127
CRANK *Minty Taylor*	133
MELA *Francesca Thesen*	136
A ROOM IN THE CASTLE *Artemis Tsatsaki*	140
THE SOUP OF SADNESS *Amelia Vale*	145
YOU'RE A DOCTOR *Isabella Winton*	148
CASSIOPEIA *Flora Wood*	153
AUTHOR BIOGRAPHIES	159
EDITORS	165

UNDERLINE

Claudia Besant

NEVERSINK

The cottage was surrounded by trees and water and animals, not another person for miles. Everything was silent, still. My window could easily have been a frame and the view a painting; it was only the slight rustle of the leaves that ruined the illusion. My Nikon, a present from my dad's guilty conscience, wasn't zooming out and I was trying desperately to fix it so I could capture the postcard view. Zac and I had decided to escape the falling debris of our parents' messy divorce and spend the rest of summer vacation at the family cottage in Neversink. The country was such a change from the frantic, noisy East Village of New York City. It was somewhere I could actually hear myself think and take *real* photos; there were only so many pigeons, gross sidewalks and looming grey skyscrapers a girl could photograph in one lifetime.

Zac was leaving for Cornell to study Anthropology at the end of vacation, so we made a pact to make the most of our trip at the cottage. Why he then decided to invite Elias Baker, I have no freakin' clue. This guy would call me 'Andrea' constantly. He didn't even pronounce it right. He knew it was Andy, he knew it, but he loved to see my eyes roll every time he said it. I'd seen him hanging out with Zac a bit at school but I never really thought they were that close. He was the kinda guy that showed up to a hiking vacation in an Avirex jacket, brand-new Guess jeans and fancy sneakers. A total moron.

I tossed the camera onto my bed. Geez, who was I kidding? I couldn't fix it. My eyes traced Neversink River that ran past my window and greeted the reservoir in the distance. I could've reached out and touched it, dipped my fingertips in the cool water and let it whisk me away. It had been so long since I'd seen the reservoir, I could hardly remember it. I threw on a red tee, denim overalls and a fanny pack for my Olympus. Cameras were my security blanket, I couldn't go anywhere without one.

I'd just started walking toward the reservoir when Zac called, 'wait, hold up! Where ya going? You can't go out by yourself. We'll tag along.' I rolled my eyes. He just had to play the big ol' protective brother as usual. I liked being alone. It was tiring having to impress people all the time. I wasn't like Zac. He was always surrounded by heaps of people, enjoying every second of it. He craved attention, it was his oxygen. I preferred mine a bit fresher.

'Come on, Elias, we'll catch that *Friends* episode later,' Zac said.

When Elias finally appeared, he was no longer wearing his flashy get-up, but the Knicks sweater I gave Zac one Christmas and his favourite combat boots. No way Zac would have given them to him. Elias pulled tight his red bandana, his dark hair tumbling over the top of it, and smirked as he passed in front of me. Ugh, typical.

As we reached Neversink Reservoir, the sun disappeared and bruised clouds stole the sky. For some reason I started to feel nauseous. I thought about turning back but Elias challenged Zac to a race, designating the blue flag that towered up ahead as their finishing line. They shot off like two bullets, and I lifted my camera to watch them through the viewfinder. Zac was beating him by a long shot. He looked back toward me, beaming. I laughed and went to snap a picture, but he vanished. My heart skipped a beat and I dropped my camera. He was on the ground. Elias jumped over him and grabbed the flagpole. What an asshole. I sprinted toward him. Zac's knee was badly cut but they were both laughing like total loons. I knelt down to look but he batted me away like a fly.

'Hey! Look at that old thing.' Zac pointed to a beat-up, blue rowing boat, just down the slope from the flagpole. It looked as though it had been dragged out of the reservoir and abandoned.

Elias jumped onto the front of it and opened his arms wide, gazing over the mass of water. 'I'm the king of the world. Waaahoooo!' he yelled, copying the scene from the new Titanic film everyone had been talking about.

'We so have to go out in it,' Elias grinned. 'Give it a push, dude.'

'Wait, we can't just take it, someone might own it,' I said.

Elias glared at me. 'No one owns this pile of garbage.' He jumped out of the boat and stared me square in the face. His features were sharp. He was good looking but there was something unnerving about him.

'Come on, Andy, we're only borrowing it. It'll be fun. We always used to go kayaking on the reservoir with Mom and Dad,' Zac pleaded.

I frowned. He said he wouldn't talk about them. I never used to go out with them anyhow, I was always the one watching and taking photos.

'No freakin' way.' I backed up until I bumped into the flagpole.

'Come on, Andrea. Are you seriously scared?' said Elias. 'You know how to swim, right? You can't be that much of a sissy.'

I stared at the ground and then at Zac. He didn't say anything. Elias smirked and let the silence linger.

'Fine, suit yourself,' Zac shouted. 'Give me a hand, dude.' They started to push the little boat into the water. The reservoir resisted. It had become choppy and they struggled to shove it a decent distance from the edge. I heard the whistling of an eagle and looked up into the sky. Nothing. A faint amber outlined the threatening clouds like the edge of a piece of paper that had just been set alight. I felt a pang in my stomach. I couldn't let him go out there alone with that moron. With a brief glance back from Zac, they picked up the oars and started to row away.

Wait!' I shrieked. With a small run-up, I leaped as far as I could and just managed to make the boat.

'Andy!' Zac grabbed my arm to stop me tumbling back, but I lost grip on my camera and it toppled out of my hand. I leant over the side and looked desperately into the dim, murky water. It was gone. Damn it.

'What a loser,' Elias muttered under his breath. I wanted to punch him.
The boys competed with their rowing strokes, making the boat rock even more. I felt dizzy and placed my head in my hands, focused on the floor, counting the cracks in the wood to stop the world from spinning. The wind had really picked up speed. A zingy, sweet fragrance hit my nostrils. Strange. I glanced up at Zac to see if he'd noticed that I wasn't exactly looking the best shade of human. Nope.

I was about to tell them to turn back when a sudden flash of lightening ripped through the sky and illuminated the reservoir. The boys stopped rowing, dropping the oars with a thud. A growl of thunder followed, causing my heart beat to echo through my body. The water became more and more turbulent and I grabbed the sides of the boat. I looked back at the blue flag. We were almost in the middle of the reservoir. How had we managed to get so far out?

'Err, I think we better go back,' Zac said. I nodded in agreement.

'Don't have a cow, man. It's not that bad.' Elias sounded confident but I could sense a hidden unease in his voice. Zac ignored him and smiled reassuringly at me. As he bent down to pick up the oars, the boat jerked and he was flipped over the side. I gasped and reached out to grab him but the water pushed against the boat, separating us. Elias and I flew back, hitting our heads against the wood. The wind pressed into my face with all its force, suffocating. I looked over toward Elias, his expression full of fright and panic, like a terrified child who'd lost his parents in the mall. He seized the oars and started to row back. With all my strength I managed to pull myself up.

'Where is Zac? Elias! Where the hell is Zac?' I screamed.

'He's too far away,' he yelled. I scanned the water and spotted his blonde hair in the distance.

'We can save him. What are you doing? Turn around. We can't just abandon him. Elias, stop!' Another crack of thunder. Rain started to fall from the sky. He didn't stop. I reached for the oars but he elbowed me in the stomach. And then the face. I slammed onto my back, couldn't move. I opened my mouth and cried out, choking on rain. My cry hovered in the air in front of me. It never travelled any further. A sour taste swarmed my mouth. My vision blurred and my ears rang with alarm. Everything seemed to slow but my heart raced. The rain felt like nails piercing my skin and my drenched overalls hammered me to the boat. In that moment, something within me was swept away, leaving me trembling and empty. Flashes of lightning veined the abyss above. I had to do something.

But my body didn't move. I was completely numb. I glanced in Elias' direction, but he was gone. The flagpole appeared, looming next to me. A shockwave gushed through my limbs and I jolted forward. I was safely abyss above. I had to do something.

But my body didn't move. I was completely numb. I glanced in Elias' direction, but he was gone. The flagpole appeared, looming next to me. A shockwave gushed through my limbs and I jolted forward. I was safely on land, but there was no sight of my brother. Awareness of what had just happened started to sink in. My nose began to bleed. I watched as the blood dripped onto the blue, chipped paint and became diluted by the rain. Zac was a strong swimmer, surely he'd survive this? He wasn't gone. I vaulted out of the boat and shoved it back into the reservoir. I was not going to leave him. The waves battled against me and water started to fill the boat. I screamed his name over and over, but only the thunder replied, warning me to turn back. But I wouldn't. I couldn't.

I'm looking at him now. He's there, just across the dimly lit room. He's standing next to his wife. She's beautiful. They're both laughing. The Christmas lights sparkle around them, like a scene from a fairy-tale. He lifts some mistletoe and they kiss. A proper kiss. One that makes everyone else in the room stare and envy their love.

I feel nauseous. The floor shifts beneath me. Is that really Elias? I begin to shake, with shock or anger, I'm not sure. It can't be him. I haven't seen him since that day. He didn't even bother to attend the inquest. Elias just vanished, erased himself from my life. Though he was the one who destroyed it. But it is him. He's right here, at this party, I can almost touch him. How can he just stand there like nothing happened?

I pour myself more wine, hands shaking, and watch him a second longer, my eyes locked on his face. I have to say something. I take a deep breath and step toward him. You let him die. You let my brother die. But the words never leave my mouth. I'm choking. I can see the flashes, hear the rumbling. The sour taste returns. My skin is damp. I'm frozen but trembling. My head is pounding. I did all I could. I searched for you, Zac, I did, but I wasn't strong enough. I should have run for help. Why did I think I could find you alone? If only I hadn't gone on that walk, if only I'd just stayed in that fucking cottage. Then you'd be here, with me. I lost you.

Forgive me.

Amy Bonar

'YUGTO'

> *A house in Bahrain. There is a separate Maid's Headquarters, which is attached to the house.*

ISA

NILDA: In the Philippines, we call it 'Yugto'.
    It is a change.
    A big change in our life.
    I had a very big change.
    I travelled 4995 miles. 9 and a half hours by plane.
    I left behind everything I knew
    My life
    My husband
    My daughter
    To be here.
    I sacrificed everything
    To come here.
    But so do many women.
    The agency tells us the Middle East is where we can start our lives.
    Earn good money.
    So we board a plane
    Like cattle
    To make a new start.
    A new life.

    When I got here
    I did not expect such a big house.
    It is a palace, fit for a king and queen.
    Seven bathrooms, five bedrooms.
    And everything is tiled.
    Madam wants everything perfect.
    She shouts a lot.
    She thinks I am lazy.
    But I try very hard.

DALAWA

MARYAM: Is this where you live?
NILDA: Maryam, you need to knock first.
MARYAM: Wow. It's tiny.
NILDA: Well, it's just for me.
MARYAM: My room is a hundred times bigger. And I'm smaller than you!
NILDA: Well you need a bigger room than me with all those toys you've got.
MARYAM: I guess. I definitely like my house more though. You should come and live with us.
NILDA: Habibti, I'm fine here.
MARYAM: But we've got loads of space.
NILDA: Yes, but that house is for you, your mama and baba –
MARYAM: We could play games all the time, and –
NILDA: Maryam, I like it here. It's cosy.

TATLO

NILDA: Muni-muni,
   That's what I do a lot.
   I think.
   When I'm not thinking, I pray.
   I pray that my family are safe, and happy.
   I work on my English in my spare time.
   It distracts me from my thoughts.
   I don't like to get lost in them.
   I don't want to feel more lost
   Or lonely.
   I need to remember why I am here.
   I am here to provide for my family.

APAT

MARYAM: It's Friday.
NILDA: I know.
MARYAM: Why are you here?
NILDA: I've got to clean the house.
MARYAM: But this is your day off.

NILDA: I've got to clean the house.
MARYAM: I wouldn't want to be cleaning on my weekend. I'll ask Mama and Baba to let you go.
NILDA: It's fine. Habibti, why don't you go and play, okay?

MARYAM: Are you sure you don't want me to ask?
NILDA: Mama and Baba are having a party tonight. They need the house extra clean. That's why I'm here. I don't mind.
MARYAM: You're sure you don't mind? Pinky promise cross your heart and hope to die?
NILDA: I pinky promise cross my heart and hope to die.

LIMA

NILDA: I am supposed to have Fridays off.
    It is rest day.
    But sometimes Madam and Sir make me stay.
    Some weeks, I have no breaks.
    And that is hard.
    My back hurts.
    My body aches.
    And my hands get dry.
    So dry they start to crack.

    I do not say anything.
    But bodies need rest.
    I need rest.

    Bahrain is all dust. There's no green like Manila. No colour.
    But it is nice to go out.
    Sometimes I'll go to the Shawarma shop, or I will get a bus to the Souq and just walk around.
    It's nice to leave the house.
    And sometimes I will go with the other maids from the compound.
    We all talk about our lives. For hours.
    Our lives here and back home
    Some of them work for very kind people.
    Others are not so lucky.
    But we all miss home.
    I like being with them.

Stops me from feeling lonely.
So when they take my Friday away from me
I am angry.
When a little girl can see that it is not okay
But grown adults seem to think that it is fine
Then I just do not understand.

ANIM

MARYAM: Why did you want to be a maid?
NILDA: So I can get money. It is a job.
MARYAM: But there must have been other stuff you wanted to do?
NILDA: I don't know. I don't think about it.
MARYAM: Even when you were a little girl? Did you never dream of being a ballerina?
NILDA: I did always want to be a teacher.
MARYAM: So why didn't you do it?
NILDA: I left school. No qualifications.
MARYAM: Why did you leave school?

NILDA: I had to leave, when I was a little girl. Around your age.
MARYAM: Why?
NILDA: I had to support my family.
MARYAM: Didn't your mama and baba give you pocket money?
NILDA: They didn't have enough.
MARYAM: But why did you come here?
NILDA: No work in the Philippines. So I came here. Better pay. I came here to make money to keep my daughter in school. Make a better life for my family.

PITO

NILDA: I just want to be 'alpas'.
   To be free.
   If I could be a bird, I would fly back to my country, fly far, far away from here, from the Middle East.
   I would be free.
   Free of madam and sir.
   Be with my family.

Cradle Erma in my arms.
See her smile.
My little ray of sunshine.
But I can't afford a plane ticket,
Not on my salary.
40BD a month, and I send most of it back home.
But if I was bird, then that wouldn't matter.
I would be with them now.
It would all be okay.

WALO

MARYAM: Do you have a husband?
NILDA: Yes.
MARYAM: Do you love him?
NILDA: Yes.
MARYAM: I'm not sure that mama and baba love each other.
NILDA: Of course they do, don't say that.
MARYAM: If you're in love, you would talk to each other all the time. And I never see them talking.
NILDA: That's not true. And they love you very much, and that's what matters.
MARYAM: They don't talk to me.
NILDA: Yes they do –
MARYAM: No they don't. They pretend to listen but they're not really listening. Maybe I'm just boring.
NILDA: You are not at all boring.
MARYAM: But you're my friend. You actually like talking to me. Do you have any kids?
NILDA: Yes.
MARYAM: Are they naughty?
NILDA: I have a daughter. She's a bit of a troublemaker, just like you.
MARYAM: She's an only child?
NILDA: Yes.
MARYAM: That's just like me!
NILDA: And she's your age as well.
MARYAM: What's her name?
NILDA: Erma.
MARYAM: Erma. That's a funny name. Do you miss her?
NILDA: Yes.
MARYAM: At least you've got me though.

NILDA: Yes, my little ray of sunshine.
MARYAM: You should go back for a holiday and see them.
NILDA: Who would tidy up your messy bedroom?
MARYAM: I could keep it tidy! I'm really good at making my bed.
NILDA: You are.
MARYAM: It would make you happy going back, wouldn't it?
NILDA: Yes.
MARYAM: You should go soon. Just as long as you'd promise to come back.

SIYAM

NILDA: Sir hit me.
   The other day.
   On my face.
   I can cope with that.
   Men are like that, they get angry.
   I understand.
   But yesterday I felt his eyes on my back.
   Just watching me.
   Silently staring.
   I didn't know what to do.
   Maybe he'd hurt me again.
   Do I run? Cry for help?
   I keep cleaning
   But He is just staring
   And then I feel him coming closer to me
   His warm breath on my neck
   Breathing deeply
   Smell of alcohol and shisha

   It makes me sick
   He makes sick

   He still says nothing
   Edging nearer to me
   Circling me like I'm an animal
   Pinches my bum
   Rubs his hands up and down
   Breathing heavy

   I feel sick.

I am sick.

How can a husband, and a father do that?
In the eyes of God? His wife? Or his daughter?
In his eyes, I am a piece of meat. His prey.

SAMPU

MARYAM: What's the Philippines like? You never talk about it.
NILDA: Well, it's very colourful, there's lots of trees, and tropical fruits...
MARYAM: Do you like it more than here?
NILDA: It's different.
MARYAM: Can I go there one day?
NILDA: I'm not sure your mama and baba would like that.
MARYAM: Why not? You could take me there. Please!
NILDA: Okay, we'll see.
MARYAM: Do you think you'll ever go back?
NILDA: Someday.
MARYAM: When is 'someday'?
NILDA: I'm not sure.
MARYAM: Do your family not want to see you anymore, is that it? Is that why you never go back?
NILDA: No, it's not like that. I'm saving up.
MARYAM: Oh. When will you have enough money?
NILDA: Soon.
MARYAM: You never spend any money though.
NILDA: I do.
MARYAM: But you never go out.
NILDA: Well –
MARYAM: You've been saving for ages. How can you not have enough money?
NILDA: Flights cost a lot of money, its half way around the world –
NILDA: Maryam, shall we play another game?
MARYAM: Do you not get enough money here?
NILDA: Yes, Maryam, yes – look, let's play another game of snap, I can't let you go on beating me.
MARYAM: Do Mama and Baba not give you enough money?
NILDA: Yes, Habibti, they do.
MARYAM: I can ask Mama and Baba to give you more money, you should go home and see your family –
NILDA: No, Maryam, please don't do that. They give me enough.
Remember when I told you that I'm sending a lot of my money back home?

To my family?
MARYAM: Yes.
NILDA: Well, that's where most of my money is going.
MARYAM: Oh. Well they must be really rich now. If I was you, I would want to keep it all to myself.
NILDA: They need it more than me. Come, let's play another game.

LABING-ISA

NILDA: Sir scares me.
   I walk around this house in fear.
   Maybe I should report him.
   But what good does that do?
   Who will listen?
   They will laugh.
   Better to stay silent.
   I haven't got long to go.
   Maybe a year or so.
   I can last a year. Can't I? I have lasted this long.

   Do not let them see your rage.
   They can do bad things, keep me here.
   Take away my passport.
   They could make me suffer.
   Kafala Law.
   That's why they treat us like dogs, if they want.

NILDA: Maryam, I'm going to go home soon.
MARYAM: When do you leave?
NILDA: In a few months.
MARYAM: So you saved up enough money?
NILDA: Yes.
MARYAM: When are you coming back?
NILDA: I'm not coming back. I'm going home, for good.
MARYAM: What? Why? Have I done something wrong?
NILDA: No, not at all.
MARYAM: Then why are you leaving me?

NILDA: I need to go home.
MARYAM: Can't this be your new home?
NILDA: Maryam, I can't stay here forever.
MARYAM: But I don't want you to go. And I'm your family too. You can't leave me.
NILDA: Maryam, I'm your maid. Your family are here. My family are far away. I need to be with them.
MARYAM: But I love you, Nilda. You're my best friend. Please, please, please don't leave me.
NILDA: You're going to be fine. You can call me, okay? And you are going to have a nice new maid, who will play games with you too. Okay? It will be fine.
MARYAM: She won't be as nice as you.
NILDA: She will. I'm sure of it.
MARYAM: I'll miss you.
NILDA: I'll miss you too.
MARYAM: Pinky promise cross your heart and hope to die that you'll call?
NILDA: Pinky promise cross my heart and hope to die.

They embrace.

Black-out.

A young girl walks on stage, wearing a uniform.

MAID: In the Philippines, we call it 'Yugto'.
   This is a change.
   A big change.
   A Scary change.
   I have left behind everything.
   I do not know what to expect.
   I feel alone.
   I am scared.

   Black-out.

Daniel Box

RESTART FROM LAST CHECKPOINT?

We huddle round to interrogate barren
hourglasses, choking sand and upon
the dust pondering, whilst off the starboard
bow horizon tsunamis echo ten
clicks off, ignore the T-minus klaxons,
ignore the klaxons and screw your eyes shut
tightly to block out the blades lurking in
the branches, prowling like ravenous wolves.

Ignore the quartz equine throne, a pearly
Radiance outshone by no earthly glow,
Upon which beside the zero reclines
Its marrow bow. Its thunderous gallop
Echoes through Chaos like a great gong
Discordant. Ignore the first vault unlocked.

Ignore the crimson legion, whose four hooves
Crack the clay like sadistic battering rams,
Upon from which the Black Surgeon surveys
The wreckage of the final Golden Age.
Femur sword raised in salute, beckons pain
Blood-drenched. Ignore is the second vault unlocked.

Ignore the shadowed mounts, from deep within
The Politician protrudes, unblemished,
Carcasses expelled with every breath
Intake, breast clutch the gilded Plenty Scales
Unbalanced, wheat burns belching soot into
The star dome. Ignore the third vault unlocked.

Ignore the spectre, ignore the starving
Oesophagus, ignore the cleansing blade
Of Tartarus unleashed upon the plains

Infernal, sweeping cull of the pale horse
And Hell in unholy matrimony.
Cold Hades, Ignore the fourth vault unlocked.

We leave this all behind to flee to stars
Distant, to regress to lone voices in
The night, each a fading echo of a
Dream long sullied by the dirt, each a hope
Lost to the quicksand, each desperately
Yearning to forget that, even across
Dark space, our shadows refuse to stray from
Our smoke eternal shrouded, rotting wakes.

Ignore the far flung comets circling
High above the mortal plane, whilst choked cries
Echo through the wind like whispers, wailing,
Begging for avengement, for some divine
Judgement to descent upon this realm like
Starving Hawks, ignore the fifth vault unlocked.

Ignore the star dome, wherefore Luna bleeds
And Helios is slain and the stars go out
Like candles in a storm. For the first time
Since the Dawn, he closes his eyes tight shut
And Olympus retreats and rolls away like a
Wayward wave, ignore the sixth vault.

Behold the sons and daughters of the end,
Of the final shadowed transgression, who
First were cast out of bountiful Eden,
Now are cast out of the barren Wasteland
And shelter under dark Himalayan
Expanse. We tearful watch the seventh vault
Remain locked.

We still cower from the night.

Martha Boyd

COME HOME JETHRO

O brother, did you go to San Francisco
without me?
      Our 'Slow Rollercoaster City'
           sculpted out of dreams,
             photographs

    I think your postcard must be lost,
are you?

I imagine San Francisco smells of chocolate,
        But remember, so does York
          for when you want to come home

Are you gay in San Francisco? I hope so,
      I feel like you've always wanted to be

                 Mum and Dad say hi
           sorry they can't say it themselves
        you know how hopeless they are...
     I hope that's not why you've gone

Are you looking into the harbour
        telling people 'the water's laughing, not lapping
            because the seaweed's awful funny you see'

      Are you looking at the sky, blotchy pink, blushing
    because he's in love with you

                too embarrassed to propose;
        don't say you're already there, clinging to a cloud.
    That's not where you've gone, is it?

Are you perching on a hill,
  close to tumbling, dying to
              roll down it until you're a patchwork
                      made of grass stains?
                Tell me which hill and we can be
                      those patchworks again
                Meet me on hill 60 and I'll even mottle
                      my wedding dress with green

        Are you homeless in San Francisco? No,
    I bet you're rich in San Francisco, although
  I hope you haven't been betting, again
I really hope you're okay

Have you formed your own jazz band
                in San Francisco?

            Do you work in IT?
      Are you keeping up to date on me
using the friendliest of spyware?

  Sounds like that pays well, so,
      surely you can afford to come home
            soon, Jethro

      I decided to move into the airport
    I shop for groceries without paying
  See, I don't work in IT,
my unpaid internship is looking for you

You're a lost case
                that never turns up
                                in baggage collection

                        Does the streetcar roll by
                  screaming:

Oh-oh-ohhhh-oh

Woe, brother,
    ~~From~~ Love me,
        Grieving Rollercoaster City,
                With tears thudding like falling sky-scrapers.

            They tell me you're not in San Francisco
        That you only remain
     in my head
I could end on a couplet, but to me, you're in our city.

Felicity Brown

BOYS

Sophie opened her eyes and looked down at the arm wrapped around her waist, the fingers entwined with her own, and felt the warmth rising up into her chest. The tiny single mattress wasn't big enough for the both of them, but they pressed close to each other and held on. She could feel her heart pounding inside her chest, little beats of excitement sparking through her veins. She could feel the heartbeat in the arm around her waist, too. It was steady, calm, like the gentle strum of rain at night, endless and reassuring. She closed her eyes again and let herself sink into the rhythm of that beat, let the steady *ba-dum ba-dum* overtake her own.

She had always liked boys, but she wasn't sure that they had always liked her. When she was seven she had played with the little boys on her street in the back garden of her neighbour's house. She had sort of just assumed that she was one of them. She hadn't really seen a difference between herself and them except that out of the boys and the girls, the boys mostly had short hair. But Sophie had also had short hair at that age (her mother had perched her on the kitchen table and given her a less-than-stylish bowl-cut) so that point was moot anyway. Her neighbour's garden had a honeysuckle hedge wrapped around it and terracotta herb pots by the back door. The little lawn had been edged with daisies in the summer – their aroma and bright colours softly framing Sophie's memories. She had often played games of stuck-in-the-mud in that garden, and as a result had often fallen into the thick grass of that tiny lawn. She had pushed the boys and they had pushed her back and they tumbled happily together for years.

But when she was eleven and her mother whisked them both away from England and dropped them in the middle of Paris to 'start a new life' she found herself trying to make new friends with the boys on her new, less leafy street. There were no green gardens, only grey alleyways and roads with hard pavement. The boys were just as tough and grubby as the Parisian streets where they lived and played, and they were less inclined to associate with the little English girl whose hair had grown into little blonde plaits down her back. Sophie was just as tough and grubby as they were, but she wore it under layers of yellows and pinks, which they despised her for. The first time she had tried to talk to them, she had walked up with her hands in the pockets of her little pink corduroy dungarees and had asked to join in with their games. They had laughed at her and called her *Goldilocks*. Her face had burnt red and she had stomped away from them with a lump in her throat. Later that day she had taken the heavy scissors from her mother's sewing basket and hacked off the blonde plaits that had separated her from the boys. She had felt a swelling satisfaction in her belly as she watched them fall onto the mint green bathroom tiles. She had gone back to the boys the next morning with her hair as short and messy as theirs, but they had still laughed at her. One boy with soft green eyes had shoved her onto the rough concrete pavement, ripping her dungarees. He towered over her.

'You're ugly now.' He spat.

She watched him walk away, her palms stinging, and wished she knew how he was different from her. She had stayed away from them after that, watching their games from her bedroom window instead. Most weekends they played football in the alleyway between her building and the next. She could peer out the window and see from the skips at the end of the alley all the way to the café on the corner.

She had been watching them play one evening, the sunlight slowly slipping away behind the lead-covered roofs, when she noticed a girl in the building opposite. She was small and dark with frizzy black hair, and she was also watching the boys' game from her window. They had waved at each other across the boys' game and became friends just like that. They clung together. Emily had a football and they would take it out to the alleyway when the boys weren't there and teach each other how to balance it on their heads or knees. They hid the ball in Sophie's backpack and only took it out when they were right at the skip-end of the alley. They'd run into the café if they heard the boys coming, and wait there until they thought it was safe to leave. They'd sit at the back, behind the big wooden bookshelves and roll the ball back and forth between them, trapped together.

Adolescence changed things. The boys were still hostile and unreachable, like some exclusive society for the now deep-voiced and lanky youth, but now they wanted something from the girls other than fear. There was a new game to be played. The other girls wore their hair long, so Sophie had grown hers out too, even though she preferred the way the boys' hair looked – with soft quiffs and shaved sides. Emily had let her hair get longer, too, and it stood up in fluffy bunches on top of her head, effortlessly. Sophie's hung limply over her shoulders, so she had taken to pulling it back into the same two plaits that she had abandoned as a child. They attracted a different attention from the boys, now.

When she was fourteen she dropped her pen on the floor during a science lesson. She had noticed the pen rolling to the edge of her desk a fraction of a second too late to catch it, but had lunged forward anyway. The pen hit the floor with a clatter, and her face hit the desk with a smack. She had straightened back up, without the pan and her forehead smarting, to see a boy with bright red glasses watching her. He had seen everything and was silently laughing from across the room. He tossed her a pen, she caught it and smiled awkwardly back. For a moment she was on the same page as one of the lanky, confident creatures she had been watching since girlhood. She clutched onto that moment. When, a month later, he had kissed her, it only seemed fair to kiss him back. She was grateful to be near the exclusive society, even if she wasn't allowed over the threshold, and Marc had brought her right up to the door. He had offered her a space at the table for girls-who-were-*with*-boys and she needed to adjust to being one of those honoured VIPs. She learnt how to reapply makeup during breaks, how to style her long hair, how to fade into the group of girls who watched from the sidelines as their scruffy, athletic boyfriends kicked a ball and flexed their muscles. She would watch and picture herself out on the field with them, her hair shaggy and pushed out of her face as she skipped lightly over the ball and snatched it away from their grasp. Sometimes they let her kick the ball about with them, and Marc told her she was *adorable*. She was so close to them, but so distinct and separate; they would play 'girls versus guys' games where the boys teamed up against their girlfriends and guffawed at each other over how they were *caniches* for letting the girls score. She played along and missed the goals so they wouldn't think she was trying too hard. That wouldn't be cute. And she needed to be cute to be near them.

When she was sixteen she cut her hair short again. Not in her bathroom with her mother's scissors this time, but at a salon, with a picture of Brendon Urie clutched in her hand. If she could have short hair, then so could Sophie. She satin the plush chair and felt the excitement fizz through her chest as the hairdresser snipped away atthe limp plaits. She felt lighter without them.

Marc had told her that she looked 'boyish'. He said it like it was a bad thing, with his head to the side and a grimace as he held a few strands between the tips of his fingers. Like it made her too much like him. Like it made her less pretty. Less of a *girl*. She remembered the boy with soft green eyes towering over her and felt the anger creep up into her throat. He had been beautiful. Marc was beautiful. Brendon Urie's picture, lovingly crumpled in her pocket, was beautiful. And now that she looked more like them, she was ugly. Her cheeks had flushed red and she walked away from him without a backward glance.

Emily's eyes had grown wide with admiration when she saw Sophie. She had taken her by the hand, her touch soft and electric, and had sat her in front of the big mirror in her mother's room. She had insisted on styling Sophie's new hair every way imaginable, and her excitement inspired Sophie's more and more, until they were dancing around the bedroom, blasting out Queen and Bowie and screaming the words out of tune. They were pelting out *I Want to Break Free* and Emily had jumped onto her mother's bed to scream,

'GOD KNOWS I'VE FALLEN IN LOVE!'

Sophie looked over at her, her frizzy black hair bouncing on top of her head, and felt the excitement change from effervescence into relief and warmth. It spread through her chest and into her tummy, bursting and sparking like fireworks. She leapt onto the bed as well and they spun around together, bound up in the ecstasy. Sophie's hair fell into her eyes and she shook it back. She ran her fingers through it and laughed at how easy it was to push aside.

'*This is it,*' she thought, and took a mental snapshot of the moment.

The dinky single room was filled with light. Sophie could see it through her eyelids, but she kept them shut to preserve the illusion of sleep. She knew if she opened her eyes she would see all of the luggage she'd dumped onto the floor the previous evening, and if she saw it she'd have to acknowledge its existence and deal with it. The arm was still wrapped firmly around her waist, and she could still feel its steady and calming rhythm beating against her fingertips. *Ba-dum, ba-dum, ba-dum.*

'I've got to break free-ee,' Sophie murmured. Emily snorted and withdrew her arm.

'LORD KNOWS I'VE GOT TO BREAK FREE!' She retaliated, loud enough to wake the entire residential hall. Sophie tried to shush her but fell off the tiny mattress as she rolled, pulling the blanket off with her. She lay on the hard floor, laughing at her own clumsiness. Sophie could feel the edge of her suitcase digging into her ribs as she laughed, and the maroon carpet from the 70s scratched at her spine. Emily stood over her and pulled her to her feet. She pushed Sophie's quiff back from her eyes and brushed her lips against her forehead.

'You look like James Dean today. Like, if he was blonde.' Emily announced

Sophie grinned. 'That's what I'm going for.' She said.

She still liked boys. But she liked Emily much, much more.

Sophie Bunce

A FIFTY PERCENT CHANCE OF A FUTURE

Alex has been thinking about kissing Louise for the last half an hour. He can't help it. He wonders what her hair feels like and what toothpaste she uses because Louise looks like a Colgate girl; but who can tell these days? He wonders if he'll ever find out, between watching the way she adjusts her glass, shifting it left to right every few minutes. As she talks, he notices that her eyes are just a little too big. She has a pretty symmetrical face and a pretty nice smile. She seems funny, intelligent and all of the other dating website buzzwords that made Alex swipe right. As she sits across the table, arms uncrossed, he can't help but think she is way out of his league and that if they ever have children he hopes they get her eyes so they can see better in the dark. But for some reason she likes him.

He realises, about 5 minutes too late, that Louise has been talking while he was thinking about her eyes and her toothpaste. She has been talking and thinking while he was just staring. She is asking for a response.

'So, what would you do? Would you say yes or no?' she says.

Alex looks at her blankly. For her question, there is a fifty percent chance of success. Yes or no, right or wrong. His gut says go for yes because the answer is almost always yes. But the answer is also almost always no.

'No?' he says.

'Oh' she says. Her arms cross.

The crossing of her arms makes Alex's heart sink. He is wrong. He regrets this no more than almost any other no he has ever said. In the history of *no's* it is just before the no that left him with salt free chips yesterday and the no to kissing Sally Bradwick in Year 10. Sally Bradwick was a 10/10 in year 10. But now she's a strong 7 so he doesn't think of her much.

'Fuck off!' he says to himself.

Louise's eyes widen and she adjusts her pony tail, flicking it side to side, uncomfortable with the way it sits, uncomfortable with the way she sits. Her arms tighten around her torso as she makes herself as small as possible in the chair. She thinks he was talking to her. The sweet, calm man was mean and she doesn't know what to do. 'No, sorry, I meant me. Um, I wasn't telling you to fuck off. That would be awful. I was just... Uh... talking to myself then' he explained, pointing at his head.

Alex realises admitting you talk to yourself is no better than telling your date to fuck off. Lesson learnt, but too late. Her eyes won't quite meet his, it's like she's looking for someone behind him, and he watches all his first date work fall away. There will be no lingering looks, no slow goodbyes. He didn't even know if he *liked her*, liked her yet. After half a date he was not ready for the double like. But he did know that with her a Tuesday evening felt like the weekend and Alex loves the weekend.

He asks for the bill. Their deserts are finished, they didn't share any, and he thinks that she's ready to leave even though she hasn't said a word. The napkins are unused, neither put them on their laps. At first Alex thought this was sweet. Maybe their mutual lack of manners meant that they were compatible. After all, the girl he went out with a few months ago always put her napkin on her lap at dinner and she was awful. Like, mocked him because he couldn't use chopsticks awful and said that people who drove Skodas were poor, awful. Alex doesn't have a Skoda but he liked the possibility that he could, so he thinks of her even less than Sally Bradwick, the once 10/10 from year 10. He thought these napkins had potential, that Louise had potential. That one day they could have been a proper couple who fight about her mother, using a Tesco clubcard and the winner of Eurovision. But now the napkins were just folded reminders of what could have been. Reminders shaped like patronising swans.

It has been minutes since they last spoke. Full minutes. In the quiet, Alex has been thinking about the restaurant. Maybe he picked wrong. Maybe that's why everything is wrong. He chose a venue close to her house because Louise mentioned she liked to wear heels and Autumn hadn't hit yet so it was warm at night. The walk home was going to be romantic. They would have discussed current events and laughed at how far worries of mortality feel when you're on the cusp of love. But no luck. He'd never learn what toothpaste she used. Instead, Alex wondered if he should offer to get her a taxi. Does she call them taxis or cabs? A lot of English people had picked up the Americanism of cabs. Another thing he'd never know.

'Alex, fuck off.'

'What?' Alex looked up from his palms and across the table at Louise.

'Fuck off.'

'Ok, I'll go. Sorry... uh' he shifts in his chair preparing to leave.

'I'm joking. Don't go. Sorry, I just wanted to diffuse the tension. It was all going well and then you made it weird. Let's start again. We can start from my question. Who would you punch if you could punch anyone and who would you want to be punched by? Would you do it?' she says, sitting forward and propping her elbows on the table, her chin resting on her hands.

Alex frowns. This is her question? This is the decider? This is the stupid question that is going to keep her big eyes in his little life? Until ten secondsago he had written off any hope of a second date. He was awkward, she was wonderful and their date was in past tense. He was already preparing the way he'd tell his mates that she wasn't his type or that he didn't like the way she said 'economics' so it could never have worked. But now, she is asking him a question and the answer will matter. Properly matter. Not matter like they told you your GCSE's would but actually mean something. But time is running out and he needs to answer. He has already been staring and thinking for far too long and once again the only thing going through his head is toothpaste. When he thinks about punching someone, the guy that hit on his now ex-girlfriend immediately comes to mind. He hadn't realised that still made him angry but thinking about it made Alex ball his fists at the table. Then he thought, that maybe, he would choose to punch himself. He could punch himself and be punched by himself. If he had two bodies he could make them punch each other to teach themselves a lesson. Alex wonders who would win. Surely he can't say any of that? That sounds mad. Perhaps he could make something up. But Alex is not sure, not sure at all, because her slightly too big eyes have caught him in an unwavering stare.

So he begins his answer. Louise sits forward in her chair and adjusts her placemat as he talks. He thinks he is losing her. She straightens the mat and then the napkin and stops. He still talks. She tilts her head to the right. She tenses her hands. They move to grasp the strap of her bag, knotting and unknotting it in her lap. Her eyes follow his lips. She taps her foot, her high heel clicking against the floor, her eye contact strong. He looks worried. His eyebrows are low on his forehead but hers are raised. Then it begins to grow. Her tentative smile grows. If it was a child, her smile would be afraid of the dark and check under its bed before going to sleep. But it matures, every moment becoming bolder until she is beaming across the table at him, laughing.

Louise uncrosses her arms.

Chloe Crowther

SHE AND HER

Her old self just stepped out from the mirror one day. That was the only way she could describe it – honestly, that's what had happened. She had not come from behind the mirror, for how could she, possibly, when it was hanging on the wall? Still, she reasoned, her past self was like a ghost, although she was still very much alive; that version of her no longer existed, was consigned to memory and pain and regret. So it was only logical – if such a word could even be used in this bizarre scenario – that the ghost of her former life had come from the mirror.

And there *she* was.

Her past self looked her up and down; a slow, malicious smile spread across her lips. Those were *her* lips... *had* been her lips. They were chapped in all the right places. There was even the cold sore she developed when she was stressed, just to the right of her lower lip.

'What do you want?' she found herself asking, as if this were the most natural situation in the world... as if she was confronted by her time-travelling past persona every Thursday.

But her past self was not forthcoming. Instead, she simply continued to smile, so her present self reasoned that – well, that she had a lot on her To-Do list for today, and that, if her past self wasn't going to disrupt her schedule, she may as well get on with the minutiae of her daily routine.

At present, she lived in a semi-detached townhouse in a good neighbourhood; the council collected the bins every Monday and on alternate Thursdays, the 20-mile-per-hour speed limit was adhered to (this being a school district) and there were lots of local green spaces. In fact, she now worked in the park at the top of her road.

And that was her first stop for today.

Glorious sunshine played with her hair, turning it auburn at the roots. She swayed her arms, and disturbed the molecules of air into a breeze beneath her armpits. It was the perfect temperature. She could taste the honeyed elderflower cordial at the back of her throat already.

Yet there was her past self, skulking behind her; dawdling deliberately to make her present self late, no doubt! And just like the woman she used to be, too. How glad she was that that was all in the past... except the past was here, now, presently scuffing a pair of perfectly good brogues (stolen, no doubt) against the pavement.

She would never have been able to afford a pair of shoes like those.

'Hurry up!' she found herself barking, the irritation scratching at her throat, snuffing out the remembered taste of elderflower.

Eventually they made it. She pushed open the café door; the bell above was tickled into life. Her boss smiled up at her. The radio and the chatter of customers, even the hiss of steam from the coffee machine faded into the background. Sunlight dappled the translucent form of her past self, but fortunately she seemed to be the only one who could see *her*. She didn't feel able to cope with any questions.

Her past self appeared to be enjoying her new role as poltergeist; she proceeded to spend the next four hours spooking the customers, ruffling hair, swiping discarded sunhats from the backs of chairs and pelting them across the empty tables. One particularly close call had involved a pram inexplicably pushing itself (at a dangerous angle) down the disabled ramp. Exhausted, her present self fanned her armpits and tried not to cry.

When they left the café at quarter past two she hadn't even had her elderflower cordial.

This was crazy! This entire situation was an unfeasible nightmare! However, the stench of her own copious puddles of perspiration told her that this was not a fantasy.

Twirling on her heels, in the middle of the park she yelled 'Why are you here? Why are you tormenting me?!'

The past version of herself continued with that evil little smile, clearly amusing herself by staying silent. Behind this spirit, the red gingham curtains of the café twitched; so, her boss was watching her (very public) mental breakdown, too.

Well. That settled it.

She was no longer *that* person, and she was going to prove it, if that's what the whole point of this – this *torture* of an experiment was.

She took a deep breath, and closed her eyes.

'Come on then,' she murmured, much calmer now, 'We have to collect our son from nursery.'

They took the bus. Although she'd loved to drive, before, she found that it still felt like freedom, being able to pay for her own ticket and to carefully select her bus seat. She had to choose two next to each other, then she worried that people would stare at them. Thankfully no-one did, and she began to suspect that actually no body but her could see the apparition that shared her cold sore. Still, she found herself rehearsing a speech in her head, about a long-lost identical twin sister, separated at birth. Just in case.

People, old and young, tall and short, squabbled like seagulls over chips in the playground. Amongst the chaos she momentarily lost sight of the past self, but she couldn't concentrate for long enough to find her again because her little boy was throttling towards her; both tiny feet slapped against the pavement, almost launching his entire body forward into the air in his haste to reach his mother's outstretched arms. Laughing, she hugged him to her, kissing him and cuddling him, gulping in that reassuring baby smell. At least she still had him; so her past self coming here hadn't altered her present, at least not in any dramatic sense.

But how had she managed it? The woman wondered, as she heated up pasta for her son. Staring into the microwave, she thought about how gypsies read tea-leaves, and that maybe the peas and chicken chunks could reveal the divine purpose of it all to her. Screwing up her eyes, she tried to focus, but the *ping!* at the end of the timer distracted her.

The past self behaved well throughout the rest of that afternoon, however she seemed to hate bath time as much as the woman's son. An ear-splitting cacophony of wailing drove the poor woman insane that night; so much water splashed on the floor that when she finally got him to bed and went downstairs, she was rained on.

At about eight o'clock – after towelling her hair dry – the woman sat at her kitchen table; nursing a mug of camomile tea, she mulled it all over.

So. The facts, as far as she could establish them, were that an apparition of her former self had come forwards in time through her bedroom mirror. It was Thursday, but it was not a Bin-Collection Thursday. No-body else could see this past self but her, and this past self maybe couldn't speak (or maybe she was just winding her up). Today was a fine summer's day in early June, and it had not rained, nor had there been any kind of lightning storm that had somehow propelled her former self into her present.

Yet she was an everything-happens-for-a-reason kind of woman; prison had taught her that. If not to be punished, then why, after all, would she have gone to prison? Therefore, there had to be a motive behind her own sadistic, Dickens-esque visitation, too.

However, this was where she got stuck, and where her husband found her later, her head in her hands, when he returned from work at 10pm. At first, he was distressed to see his wife so unhappy – but later, when they were snuggled up on the sofa and she had explained it all to him, he became puzzled. Her husband was a solicitor, and a Cambridge alumnus. It took a lot to confuse him.

Finally, after a period of silence, he said 'Do you think it's possible, that she came here to remind you of just how far it is that you've come along?'

They were both quiet as they let this idea sink in.

In the morning, the past self was gone.

The woman checked everywhere, even in the bath (although the past self had made her dislike of bathing explicit the previous night).

Why and how it had all happened would remain a mystery forever. But life was like that. Although the woman was a believer in some version of Divine Purpose, she was not one to pontificate the meaning of it all from her armchair. And there were bills to pay, and her son needed breakfast, and her emails were starting to pile up, and of course, next Monday, she had to put out the bins...

Grace Curtis

TIGER TIGER

'Wanna go through the park?'

Alison doesn't want to, but by now she's spent enough time with Chloe to understand this isn't a question. She has a way of hardening her eyes when she smiles that means 'we're doing what I say'. Alison's seen the same dark magic exercised on the other girls at school: 'Wanna draw a dick on the whiteboard?', 'Wanna climb up the bike shed?', 'Wanna steal Nathan's glasses?'

It's all just banter, really. But then again, if you say no, what kind of person are you? A pussy at best. At worst, a snitch. Dangerous things to be. So nobody says no, and the wheels of chaos roll on.

Alison isn't one of those people, though. She isn't one of anybody. She's a non-person, a social chameleon. She sits in the middle, she doesn't raise her hand and she barely speaks.

But all of those efforts to disappear – all those years spent hiding in plain sight – it's been a waste. She and Chloe are walking home together.

It's hard to wrap her head around. Even though they share a bunch of classes, they had spoken for the first time only a couple of weeks ago. Well, no. It hadn't been speaking. Alison had been walking to class alone while Chloe's gang passed in the opposite direction. She didn't see danger coming until it was too late, didn't see Chloe's eyes fixed on her from ten yards away. Chloe had waited until the last moment, just as they passed each other, then she leapt out and screamed into Alison's face.

Alison had leapt back, raising her arms like a shield. When she lowered them, Chloe and her friends were all laughing hysterically, mimicking her startled reaction. Of course: that was the game. Alison had seen them do it to others since, but she was clearly one of their favorites. She'd trained herself to stay relatively still now, but she couldn't keep from flinching. That was more than enough for them. The scream wasn't even the worst part: it was the anticipation. Moving through the corridors with her head bowed, combing the black grey crowds for a flash of Chloe's frazzled red hair. It reminded her of a poem they'd studied in English:

Tiger tiger, burning bright
In the forests of the night

It wasn't just the hair. Chloe did everything she could to look different, striding around school in a too-tight skirt with makeup all over her pale, freckled face. Before all the bad stuff started Alison had often caught herself gawking at her in class, hypnotised by the way she pulled her cardigan apart thread by thread.

Mr Fryer said the point of the poem was that the narrator loved the tiger as much as he feared it. Alison privately disagreed.

Her reaction the first time invited experimentation with more games. They threw things at her in class. Pencils, rulers, whatever was around. When they ran out of stuff to throw they just jeered. 'Alison... what you writing, can I see? Come on, let me take a look...' Whatever they thought would get a rise. She'd lost her bag one lunchtime only to find it had been stuffed in the bins at the back of the dining hall. It stank for days, even after she washed it.

Once, in English, one of Chloe's friends leaned forward and cut the end of her ponytail off with a pair of scissors. When she turned to see what happened, the girl threw the hair in her face.

Alison blinked. Somebody sniggered. Then she turned and went back to work.

Mr Fryer had caught her on the way out of class. 'Do those girls ever give you trouble, Alison?' he asked, nodding to Chloe's back as she left the room.

'No sir.' she said. His tie was decorated with tiny cheetahs linking arms. They grinned at her with grotesque friendliness.

'Are you positive about that?' he asked. That had been what pissed her off. "Are you positive about that?" Dumb fucking question, sir. But she didn't say that. Instead she shrugged and backed away.

'I'm going to be late. Sorry.'

Chloe was waiting when she got out into the corridor. She stepped close, and Alison flinched. 'I knew you weren't a snitch, Alli.' she said. Her breath smelt like skittles.

Things started to change after that day. They still threw stuff at her, but not as much, and not as hard. Chloe started saying 'Hi' instead of screaming incomprehensibly. Chloe's friends picked up on it, and the nickname. 'Hi, Alli.' 'Morning Alli.' 'Hey.' A little chorus of people, talking at her like they were friends. A trap, or a game, or genuine, Alison couldn't tell, but she didn't like it. It was weirder than before.

One of them asked to copy her answers in maths. Another said she liked Alison's hairband. And now, without warning, this. Somehow she'd found herself sucked into Chloe's group on her way home. She'd stared at her feet and kept her mouth shut, letting the other girls talk over her head. But one by one they'd peeled off until it was just her and Chloe walking in silence.

'Wanna go through the park?'

'Sure.'

Of course she says sure. The only thing Alison knows about herself is that she's a coward. What she doesn't expect is for Chloe to grab her arm. But she does, leading her through a thicket of spindly trees. The park is abandoned. It's weedier than she remembers, and more littered. Some cans have been there so long the grass has grown up around them like bushes of rusty fruit. The faint scent of piss lingers beneath the wind. Alison lets Chloe guide her past the faded pinks and purples of the play park, down to the end where the field drops into the river. She has the feeling that pulling her arm away would be to yank the pin on a grenade. She knows Chloe has beat up girls before; she pushed Megan Hunter down a set of stairs for saying her mum was fat. The thing is, Chloe's mum is fat. She's one of the fattest people Alison has ever seen, and one of the shortest. She was there on parent's evening, her hair scraped up into a greasy ponytail, one fist clamped around her daughter's skinny arm as she dragged Chloe from one stone-faced teacher to the next.

She watched her all evening. Why? Perhaps they'd been watching each other.

They come to a stop at the crest of the slope.

'Hey!' Chloe says, finally letting go. 'There's something down there. I saw it yesterday.' Alison peeks over. She's right. Something unnaturally shiny glints among the weeds at the bottom of the hill. It sits just shy of the water; too bright to be a can or a bottle. The winking eye of a roused animal. She feels a twist in her stomach. Chloe looks at her.

'Wanna get it?'

Alison peers down the hill again. It's so steep it barely constitutes a slope, slick with still-wet mud from last night's rain. No path, no purchase, nothing. Of course she doesn't want to go down. There has to be an excuse, right? But, as her mind scrabbles, Alison's head shakes without her permission. Then her mouth starts to speak: 'No.'

Panic. She sounds too harsh. 'No – thank you.' No thank you? What was she on about? 'I should get home.'

'Home?'

There's a note of warning in Chloe's voice. The swish of a tail. Her eyes, which look like the bottom of two tiny green bottles, glint with a kind of angry interest. 'C'mon, Alison. Don't be such a baby.'

'I'm sorry...' she repeats. She steps backwards, but before she can clear enough distance, Chloe grabs her arm and pushes her over the edge.

It's all chaos for a second. Chloe is trying to shove her again, and she's grabbing – anything that she can hold onto – a fistfull of Chloe's jumper. The balance shifts. There's a bewildering skip in time and now she's lying at the bottom of the bank with at least a dozen bruises. Chloe is lying beside her. She says something Alison can't hear.

'Pardon, sorry?'

'I said –' Chloe gets shakily to her feet. She's covered in dirt and there's a ladder up her tights.

'– what the fuck is wrong with you?!'

She tries to kick her, but Alison scrambles backwards into the river. She's standing up and the slimy water is touching her ankles. She doesn't notice, though. Her hands have made fists. Her ears are ringing. She wants to kill the tiger.

'Why don't you just leave me alone!?'

In her head it was a reasonable question, but her voice breaks the moment she tries to speak. Even Chloe seems startled for a second.

'Because –' Chloe's face twists. 'Because you're so up your own arse, aren't you? Sitting there with your chin up, never talking to anyone. Staring all the time. You think you're better –'

'I don't.' Alison is crying. She hates herself for that. 'Nobody likes me.'

'Yeah, but –'

'You don't get it!' Alison yells over her. 'You'll never understand what it's like. Every day I wake up knowing I have to go – I have to go back to that place, and it makes me want to die. Every day I wake up and I wish I was dead. And you just – keep – doing it. You just keep doing it.'

Chloe says nothing.

'I don't understand why you keep doing it.' she says again, quieter.

'Fucking hell, Alli.' says Chloe. 'Learn how to take a joke.'

Alison falls on her with a howl.

It's not like before, after the push. She doesn't know what she's doing. There's a dim rush where her mind should be and everything has gone into her hands which are punching and clawing with single-minded desperation – kicking, too, and yanking that long, scraggly hair – all that control gone to nothing but a pure desire to destroy the thing that's been hurting her.

It's pain that brings her back. A sharp, vicious jab to the forehead, and suddenly everything stops. Her wide eyes journey from the blood on the end of her nose, dripping down onto the withered brown leaves, and up the length of Chloe's trembling arm to the rock that's clasped in her hand.

A dark brown stain spreads over the stone. Even though it seems only seconds have passed, they're both panting and caked in filth. The fight took no time at all. It's the kiss that takes forever.

Alison has seen kisses in movies lots of times. They're always in the center of the screen, framed by the light and triumphant music like it's the only thing happening in the whole world. But lots happens while she and Chloe kiss. The water gurgles softly behind them. Her forehead stings where she gashed it. Wind rustles the trees above them.

Then they break in two again. Just like that, it's over.

Walking home, Alison examines herself. She's wondering what the right thing to feel would be. There isn't any fanfare, no scrolling end credits, nothing to indicate one emotion or the other.

Chloe said she'd kill her if she told anyone. But she'd also asked if she was walking home again tomorrow.

'Of course.' Alison said. She caught herself. 'I mean, yeah. Yes.'

Chloe looked at her for a long moment. Then she shrugged, shouldered her bag and walked off back towards school, leaving Alison alone.

Alison comes to a halt at the end of the road. She stares at her hands, half expecting her skin to glow. Nothing happens. She looks up, still searching for the right feeling. Then she breaks into a run.

Ella Dorman-Gajic

SKIN OFF YOUR LIPS

I wonder if you still pull skin off your lips
between the tips of your teeth;
how you used to suck them in, gnaw and chew
until a trickle of blood seeped through.
They were cracked, blistered; but when I reached for the balm
you always refused, tearing off skin so calm
like picking off scabs that forever grew back; identical.

It was like this you would touch me; openly, compulsively.
Stroke my bare skin,
scratch my leg, pull me in, in
inside you, where I could confide in you.
Where I could hide in you.

But you would only pull me in to somehow tear me off.
Like you were the light, I the moth.

I can't begin to finish writing about you
because I feel like when I do, you will stop existing;
as if when I put pen to paper you are there, quietly listening.
And I'm taken back to the times I was reflected in your eyes;
bathing in water like it was our christening –
words of praise ridden between the bubbles,
soaked, absorbed into my pours:
you informing me of how special I was or
how special we could be,
knowing how easily to fill a girl with glee.
It was written in law, for you
carved into the stones that taught men how to woo.
It was trying to confirm something as fact
that you already knew to be untrue.

What a perfect, little, brief contradiction we were;

you watered my roots,
trod on my buds
and still bade me bloom,
alone in a darkened room.
Lying next to you, alone, in a darkened room.

Each thing done to me by you
was a cracked reflection of all you could not face up to.
You may be sharp, smart and raw
but all your self-diagnosed definitions mean nothing.
Nothing, if you can not find someone worth embodying them for.

But still, I wonder if you pull skin off your lips between the tips of your teeth.
Or if you even have lips at all, or what they could now possibly be used for,
other than having something to bite into, of course.
But the teeth that do it cannot be mine,
the bruises you blackened will fade in time,
there are still wounds I plaster to forbid you from prodding.

Because I know you could still do it, compulsively, satisfyingly.
Like pulling skin off your lips between the tips of your teeth.

Basil Eagle

NO DICE

*

> Clause I: The exchange of currency through games of chance in any public or private space, regardless of the sum in question, will hereby be prohibited.

*

This first stab at the issue made Dewitt pause as he considered the phrase 'games of chance'. Would the Grand Minister want a prohibition on forms of gambling that required talent as well? If an archer bet a fistful of coins that he could split his own arrow with a second shot, should he be caught under the glare of this law too? Dewitt made for the door to find Zimmerman, who was chiefly responsible on the National Council for quantifying and calculating the punishment of an offence, but met a journalist who had been waiting in ambush as he stepped outside his office. Dewitt hated journalists.

'Mr Dewitt, if you could spare a moment of your time, I work for the *Realm's Eye...*'

'If I could spare a moment of my time? Excuse me? It's hardly my time anyway, so why do you presume that you can waltz up to my office and have some? Kindly go away.'

Dewitt began to walk away from the man, but like a stray dog he followed behind him.

'I get it, I get it, I'm a busy man myself. But the public isn't taking kindly to today's news. Actually, there's talk of marches, demonstrations, all kinds of protest in every corner of the city, likely all over the country soon enough...'

This caused Dewitt to stop dead.

'I'm sure I don't have a clue what you're on about. You're lying to me just to see what you can dig up? Because I can get you thrown out of the building if you won't leave like a civil human being...'

The journalist chuckled with his own nasty grin.

'You think that little of me? And if Newkirk thinks he can just snap his fingers and make gambling illegal...'

The smile instantly left Dewitt's face. He motioned, and the journalist walked in and sank into a seat flanked by two large bookshelves.

'Now I know that dithering old tyrant thinks...'

'Remember where you are, please, and show some respect,' Dewitt snapped back before he could finish his thought. 'Tell me what you know. When did the Grand Minister make this speech?'

'You didn't know? He gave the speech in the press room today. And he left without answering our questions, but we're used to that by now. That's why I came here.'

'I need to know exactly what he said. Tell me.' The journalist leaned back, flipped open his notebook, and read back the Grand Minister's speech.

'How will you report on this? How will the other papers report on this?' Dewitt insisted.

The journalist gave him a blank look.

'How do you think? Anyway, I've answered your question so it's time for you to answer one of mine. Will you give your backing to the Grand Minister on this issue?' He pulled out a pen.

'I couldn't possibly comment on anything regarding the statements by the Grand Minister at this time,' returned Dewitt. The journalist rolled his eyes and persisted.

'How long have plans been underway to implement this law? Were the Judicial Chamber informed of its drafting? Does it have the backing of the administration, or, in your opinion, the public?'

'I will have to refer you to my previous comment,' Dewitt said, standing up. As he went to open the door, the journalist's demeanour quickly turned from smug to aggressive.

'Your lack of cooperation isn't helping you, or anyone, you know that?' he started, suddenly rising from his seat, 'If Newkirk thinks he can get away with this... but how can I expect someone like you to understand that...'

'I'm calling the guards now,' Dewitt replied calmly.

'Don't bother, I'm leaving,' the man scowled back, brushing past Dewitt.

As Dewitt watched him go, he felt a shudder of disgust and fear travel up his spine.

*

Councillor Zimmerman was an old and cautious man. His career proceeded the present system of government and even the title of Grand Minister. Dewitt knew that old and cautious men made for good allies.

'We can't possibly start searching the houses of every citizen for dice and cards,' the old man sighed now to Dewitt, 'not when the backlash is this great at even the suggestion of this law. The rollout will have to be gradual and tactical.'

'It goes beyond that. I'm telling you, the vultures from the press are expecting more than just protests this time. They're itching for blood, and I'm sure they aren't the only ones.'

'Be reasonable. The victims of our last conflict are hardly dead and buried.' Zimmerman said, stroking his beard as if contemplating a hard mathematical puzzle.

'What if that doesn't matter?'

'This isn't a constructive topic when we still have work to do. What else did you want to discuss?'

Dewitt licked his lips. 'We've discussed the title, the objectives, and I can see that you're working on a penalty system for these gamblers...'

Zimmerman nodded contemplatively. 'Yes, and what was the question?'

'What is gambling, exactly?'

Zimmerman let out another sigh. He rose from his seat and began pacing the office with his arms behind his back.

'I think you're asking the wrong question again, Dewitt.'

'I mean where do you draw the line? Was it a gamble to ban gambling? I'm starting to wonder more what it isn't than what it is.'

Zimmerman fixed his eyes on Dewitt, who turned uncomfortably towards the window.

'We're not playing a game here Dewitt,' Zimmerman replied carefully.

'You're interrogating me for answers when you don't even dare to say the questions out loud. Remember that I can only help you if you know how to help yourself.'

Dewitt gazed out at the city as dusk fell. Under the minute movements and flashes of light, he could sense a storm brewing. He stood up.

'You know where to find me,' he said, before walking out.

*

Two months later, the Measures Against Petty Gaming Act had matured to the eve of its conscription into law. Councillor Dewitt was sat on a bench with the rest of the National Council. He massaged his temples. Despite the best efforts of the orchestra to decorate the occasion with the delicate tones of a graceful symphony, the unmistakable sound of screams and banging from outside drifted defiantly into the chamber.

Suddenly, he heard clapping around him and stood up to join in with a big wooden smile. It was the Grand Minister, smiling and waving as he entered.

He strolled up to the podium and placed a meaty hand on either side of it.

At that moment, just as he began to clear his throat, an explosion from the second floor of the Residency shattered a balcony, sending debris and the blood of guards flying across the chamber. Glass, plaster and a severed hand landed next to Dewitt. The building creaked and groaned fantastically as more of its structure fell through the landing. A golden chandelier rattled overhead, sending shards of crystal raining onto the heads of guests. A pair of guards grabbed the Grand Minister and rushed him towards his emergency bunker. The rest sprang into action, escorting the hysterical crowd towards a separate corridor and racing upstairs to find the source of the explosion.

As Dewitt was half-pushed and half-dragged down the guards' tunnels, he felt a dread that bordered on hallucination. He had seen a General, sitting by the wall near the balcony, who had been crushed by a chunk of it. Dewitt could see the mangled remains of his legs, splayed out under the white marble, as he was rushed out. That image alone was all he could think of as they arrived at a safe room underneath the Residency.

*

Anya stared at the Broker's hands as they edged towards the pair of dice. She felt delirious with hatred. She hated the stench of the little dungeon that they kept her in, the endless shouting and cackling, the oppressive heat. But most of all, she hated the other children that sat around her in the semicircle. The children all sat in perfect silence, staring up at the unmoving Broker. The crowd had swelled in and a stack of coins corresponding to each child had been gathered on the Broker's table by a dirty, long-haired rat who served as his assistant.

Finally, the Broker's dice clattered over the surface of the table, drawing the attention of all in attendance. A silence descended at first, but the rhapsody soon broke once the dice had settled. The children were roused by the assistant. As the crowd's enthusiasm reached a fever pitch, Anya found herself staring down a gangly, pale girl. She looked towards the Broker. His face remained as emotionless as ever. Each participant was handed a small, blunt blade. Then, after what felt like an eternity, the last command left his lips in a slow and deliberate snarl:

'Begin.'

Anya inhaled sharply. Out of the corner of her eye, she could see a small boy lodge his blade into another's shoulder. She danced around, barging a man who had been standing too close to the ring who cursed and hastily retreated. Then she darted forward with her dagger raised. This had the desired effect, luring the girl into defending an attack that never came. It left her torso exposed, and in a split-second Anya seized on this opportunity by barrelling into her with weapon angled. She could hear the girl's heartbeat and feel her wince as they toppled down together. The other girl's blade clattered to the floor and she wilted underneath her.

Before Anya could catch her breath, a pair of hands shoved her back onto the floor. She glimpsed the small boy lying a few feet away from her with a blade caught in his neck and a thin layer of blood oozing out. Over Anya was his opponent. As his hands wrapped around her throat, Anya could hear the noise of the crowd growing distant.

*

>*Realm's Eye:* 'Orphan fighting ring scandal revealed.'
>*New Inquisitor:* 'Exclusive: interview with boy who dodged death at hands of Broker.'
>*Citizen's Voice:* 'Newkirk on child fighting ring: 'typical of gambling epidemic''.
>*Heart of Tomorrow:* 'New information on the Residency bombing.'

*

Somebody knocked on Dewitt's door. He opened it to find himself face-to-face with two guards and Councillor Troy.

'Come with us Dewitt.'

He complied, sensing the nature of the confrontation ahead of him. He knew that there was nothing to be done. When they finally arrived, Councillor Zimmerman was waiting in the room with his arms crossed behind his back.

'Take a seat.'

Dewitt obeyed.

'Councillor Dewitt,' Troy began, 'you have colluded with terrorists and spread falsehoods regarding the realm. What do you have to say?'

'Councillor Troy–'

'Grand Councillor Troy, I have been given new duties by the Grand Minister.' Dewitt managed a twisted smile.

'I see that things have moved even faster than I could have expected. And you can hardly blame me for trying what I tried. So the Realm's Eye is under your thumb now, too? Was the Residency bombing just another step in this little scheme as well?'

'Hold your tongue! Slander shall not be tolerated in these halls.'

'You should have taken my advice,' Councillor Zimmerman sighed, breaking his silence. 'You could have had a bright future ahead of you. You chose the wrong path.'

'I took a gamble, old man,' Dewitt replied on the brink of hysterical laughter, 'we're all gamblers in this room. The Grand Minister is quite the dice roller himself. At least I didn't gamble with the lives of children.'

'Your trial begins tomorrow,' snapped Grand Councillor Troy.

And with that, the guards seized Dewitt and led him out of the National Assembly.

Gus Edgar

THE PROCESS OF DYING

KEY: TIME FLIES LIKE AN ARROW, FRUIT FLIES
LIKE A RASPBERRY

When I was four my mother before gave birth to Will without leaving a will and she was willed to live but lives don't last Weekend I was reminded of her when the doctor gave me raspberries that she used to feed me, a vessel of not what but when I was eight brother Will ate some mud and nails and bloodied his mouth and nails and like Mother was sent to the ground Level is a nuisance as visitors in rowdy crowds come and go, a constant thrum and flow of footsteps through night to wake Was bearable but the funeral broke Father in two and I don't think he recovered, body certainly wasn't after World War Two Much for me to handle really, losing Father like that, all tat but that's that, life went on without me until I finally caught up In the world I went, I landed a job talking news and nuisances new, I knew that I wanted a job out on the field so I anchored In rancour to this bed silently screaming at stars fully-fledged, at the faces of my family whose eyes weigh down way down I felt after having no-one to fall back on after the war, no brother no mother so they looked for another, left me with my aunt You a luvly thing she would tell me, feed me loads to fatten me and rid herself of her own insecurity, in the end she couldn't Wait to load me off to boarding school, jeers for hairy legs and wonky ponytails tailed off and I welcomed work and play That I acted was as a scared little sheep and I would baa and bleat but my Aunt forgot and I only realised at the play's close To tears I was that day Charles left me though I suppose he couldn't get rid of the grief, and like me he thought I was liable To fits of mass hysteria my caretaker said when she left me in this godforsaken place to die yes she did, begging me under The thick sun I sit on the grass and watch my son play with slugs in the garden and here comes Charles now with The Times We shared together are looked through with love, looked through the napkin I kissed and gave to him, are looked through

KEY: /KI;/ ADJECTIVE – OF CRUCIAL IMPORTANCE.
'Her upbringing was a key reason for her failures at parenting and subsequent divorce'

Away everything I owned that reminded me of him, I tried to forget which I deeply regret, I'm in debt to his face or embrace The future or leave it to rot and I chose the former and then I forgot, lived life alone and lived it in grief, a big empty home Is where the hurt is, not the heart as I was reassured, after Charles left me I was stranded in a house big enough to fit four What it's worth, my Aunt says, I think your hair is perfect, and she crams some pie into my mouth but this time I don't mind Is being whispered and wispered away I can feel it now, the pills they fill me with are only numbing it and now I'm scared Of driving after the crash, stashes of therapy the melody of remember me aided me but silently I hate myself I hate myself To blame for Charles taking my daughter I oughta stop him and I'll do just that not bate and wait for my son to come back Was broken but little Ed was worse ready in red for the tread of the hearse, he's not moving please move he's not moving And tragic, the Oxford Mail put it, and I put it down to console Charles and Suzy who were sobbing into each other's arms Himself with a gun and bye-bye Father, this war will be over in no time, that was the last time I saw him and I think I knew Medication has me seeing colours funny, I prescribe colours to describe people, white is alright but black is evil I hate black Night as I laze and let Edward play with slugs in the garden and now Charles wakes me up to read me one of his segments Of oranges that my mother used to feed me, a vessel of what when but not and I'd suck on the slices til my gums were sore To it that my nurse bring Edward in earlier but she didn't, I'm old now and I still wait with weight for the sight of my son Was scorching that day I played with slugs in the garden while Mother watched on and I'll never forget the look she gave Up trying to save him as I cradled my boy and it was as if the blood had drained from his cheeks and spilled on the floor That's foiled you is you're too desensitised to death and I hate that about you and I nodded at Charles because he was right Next to my office the students were protesting Thatcher again and I had to anchor that anger again and talk scribbled signs Off the papers and Charles gives me a feeble hug because it must be the right thing to do but I know he still hates my sight

KEY: TIME FLIES LIKE AN ARROW AND TIME FLIES AND I NOW REALISE THAT AND
FRUIT FLIES LIKE AN ORANGE AND FRUIT FLIES BEYOND THE MEMBRANES OF MEMORIES UNTIL I CAN'T REMEMBER THEM ANYMORE

Weakens daily and my nurse feeds me tablets for it but we both know there's nothing to be done when life's almost done With yer article Miss but no I haven't even put pen to paper, I suppose this prose is not for me and I want to quit but I don't You dare give me those pills and I assign colours to people and the nurse in white is not white at all despite her attire Stammers too late and my car careers and rolls a droll roll to stop at rest like my boy Ed at rest and that is how I lost my first I needed to gather myself and gather his ashes and spit them out over the garden he used to play with slugs or was it worms Its way into my brain a beating drum a bleating sheep a bleeding boy oh boy a bleating drum we're out of time out of time And rosemary into the pan along with a knob of butter and leave the beef to stew while we roast these carrots ta Julia Child Was taken from me how dare he but Suzy visits me as the nurse, what a lovely lady she's grown up to be, she must be four Years I worked tirelessly as a reporter without the rapport of a loving parent, they weren't a witness to my life as a witness All this bloodshed and what for, a world at war starved of cause, Thatcher's the least of our worries when the Nazis advance Through each rank til I had anchored enough and I retired tired to live life tough and I sat in a care home and wasted away Across sea to America I last heard and I tried to contact him and Suzy or was it Sally but when I reached out he turned away Across sea to America I last heard and I thought about contacting him but I can't live with myself if I hear his or her voice Annoys a white noise of Nurse noise a manic grin like a mannequin I see her as me a woman who tried but couldn't save Ed Loved eating slugs and playing with raspberries in the garden, I hoped to see him as I die or at least expect a spectral vision Draining, light subsides but my boy Edward is not beside and darling Charles is not beside and I have no-one but that's okay To die I've lived enough to not be afraid anymore ignore the maw and its call and the deadline beeps it beeps and it beeps beep beep beep beep beep beep beep beep and there is my Father and there is my Mother Forgot to write her will but I didn't need to, I realise my life is its own will and that's alright so now I write the life I've lived with ink-soaked memories that have blotted and splotched and every comma is a heartbeat, and every full stop is its stop.

Sam Edwards

TO PAINT WITH THE BLOOD OF OTHERS

I am sitting in an armchair. The time is twelve minutes to four. There is a man standing in front of me taking photographs with one hand and gesticulating with the other. He is wearing a white shirt and his hair is gelled back. Sideburns. Slick teddy-boy cut. Toothpick. He turns and I notice that there is a rag hanging out of his back pocket.

Question: is this fashion? Or is he off to clean a few windows after we're done?

I am sitting here, sitting in an armchair. The time is twelve minutes to four and I'm holding a glass of cheap merlot. It tastes like piss. I have been here for just over an hour and twenty minutes. *Mes bras me font mal.* What do I need, I ask myself.

Nothing.

Nothing but the empty air to which we all owe our lives, and livelihoods, and lively wives. Jenson has a lively wife. Twenty three – two years older than his daughter. I am meeting Jenson for tapas later at Bowling-Gate. Is it preposterous to say tapas is limited as a cuisine? Jenson likes tapas. Jenson also likes flowery shirts, colourful ties, rolled jeans, manicures, tattoos, breath spray, chewing gum, lots of fucking chewing gum, hair-gel, small women, big boobs, blondes, blacks – though he wouldn't admit it. Food. I am hungry, so I suppose I will eat anything.

No. Not anything.

The photographer asks me to change the position of my legs and it is a relief as my left testicle was being crushed by the weight of my right thigh. I want patatas bravas. *Appétissant.* Jenson is completely and utterly tasteless. I saw him briefly the other day – what was it he said? 'Keep up the good work!' I said, 'What work?' And he mimed fucking painting. That!

Maybe I should paint him. I'd love to paint him. I could. No one would care about Jenson.

Peindre avec le sang des autres.

The time is five minutes to four. I am sitting in an armchair. This will go in the Observer I am told. They are calling me a visionary. Unconventional artist Benjamin Brisbois and his work-in-progress. Work-in-progress! I have not even begun. It has been three years since the Ten Faces. Three fucking years and still nothing. How do I hold this together? How do I top my last work? How should

I begin? It is hard work being me to be sure but I am kept busy. *J'aime mes jeux* and even people like Jenson, they are part of the game too.

My game.

So Mr Brisbois, can you tell us about your latest work? It is very big. *Yes, bigger than the Ten Faces?* Yes. *What do you think made the Ten Faces so popular?* Ha, I could not be so conceited. *Go on, your modesty is safe with us.* Aha, well I guess – I don't recall a focus on missing people in recent years – I mean ordinary everyday missing people. *You chose them at random didn't you?* Er yes, at random. *Go on.* Yes I believe that resonated with people, painting ordinary, random missing people from the national register. I think there is something eerie and also heart-breaking about it. Like seeing an ambulance; you know someone is not safe, but there is ambiguity. Like a glimpse of your own mortality. *I see, I see. Now is there anything you can tell us about the process?* How do you mean? *Well, like how do you work? Will you cut off a thumb this time? It's renowned that you used your own blood in painting the Ten Faces.* Ah no-no-no see, I used *their* blood. I put people in my paintings – quite literally actually. First I make them missing. Then the paint – you mix their blood in so there's no split. Blood when spread thickens like tar and there's this... synergy... I just can't explain.

I frown. That was interesting. Maybe I should talk to my psychiatrist.

All done now Mr Brisbois.

I smile and stand, shaking the young photographer's hand. His hand is clammy and soft. I look around the room as if seeing it for the first time. Faces of young interns and reporters. Females. Males. They are staring at me and it's as if, for a moment, they know what I did, know how I made them worship a monster. Then they begin to clap and I am safe. The photographer raises his hand, *Benjamin Brisbois everybody!* I close my eyes.

It's the greatest sensation, to paint with the blood of others. But this time I'm envisioning something more: their heads mounted on sticks, their eye-balls pierced by knives, their tongues waggling on washing lines, disembodied heads rolling along the floor, cut in half, frozen, melted like ice cream.

Maybe I should clap too.

I am leaving the building and my mind is running like a river. I want to eat. As I leave through the large shiny doors, a secretary stops me. I am told Jenson is on the line for me. I answer, smiling my thanks at the young lady.

- Jenson, hello.
- Heyyyy guy, how're you doin' this fine day?
- I am good. Just finishing up here. How are you?
- Hey swell buddy. What time are we meeting?
- Eight.

I close my eyes and put a finger to my lips.

- Jenson, I must ask you something.
- Anything Benjy!

I set the wine on a table inside and lick my lips, feeling the red stain remain.
- How would you like to be painted?

Abbey Hancock

TREASURE HUNT

The first time it happens, I am six years old.

The girl in my class with the Spice Girls pencil case and light up shoes, walks to the front for show and tell. No one shows and tells as much as she does. This time it's the new necklace her dad bought for her birthday. The necklace itself isn't much to look at – my dad would call it a *cheap piece of crap* – but she talks about it like it's worth millions. She says it's the best present she's ever had in her life. I wonder what it's like to love something that much, and so later when show and tell is over, I sneak into the cloakroom and take it from her bag. It fits perfectly in my pocket.

The rest of the day I make sure I stay with her. I like having something of hers without her knowing. I like it even more when she cries at three o'clock. She looks much prettier.

When I arrive home, I take it to my room and sit it on my bed. I still can't see its appeal, so I undo the clasp and place it around my neck. The star pendant sits on my chest and brushes my collarbone. The bottom spike makes a scratch on my skin each time I breathe. The marks it makes are ugly, and the chain itches against my neck, and I can't think of one reason why she would want to share this. I can't think of why anyone would ever want this. I can't love this.

My dad's footsteps echo up the stairs and I rip the *cheap piece of crap* from my neck and shove it inside the depths of my pillowcase. I hide the pillow under my bed.

Another time it happens I am thirteen.

A man in a grey van offers to take me home and I say yes because mum said white, not grey. I also don't mind the way he looks at me. The same way that dad looks at mum in her black dress. He asks me to light his cigarette so I take the lighter from his pocket and bring it to his face. He smokes it without thought; the clouds clash together and land on the windscreen. I wonder if he likes the taste or if it has become habit. It couldn't be the taste because the smell is like an engine left on in a closed garage. I don't care why anymore.

I don't react as he places a hand on my thigh until I look at his face. His bottom lip is trapped by a row of ill-fitting teeth and it reminds me of the cat when he dragged a half-dead mouse to the front doorstep. His teeth pressed into its body without getting blood on mum's carpet. He was a smart cat. I wonder what it feels like, biting down like that. I place my hand on the man's thigh and gnaw my lip too. I mimic the 'fuck' he whispers. He drives thirty seconds more before he drops me back onto the pavement. I'd never paid much notice before, but now I don't like the taste of my lip.

The lighter sits heavy in my hand. When I make it home, I slip it down the front of my vest as mum speaks to me.

'How was your day, love?' She asks. She blocks both the entrance to the kitchen and the stairs. I've never resented my mother's size until this moment. I pick at my sleeve and stare at her feet. Her ankles roll over themselves, and create layers. Layer on layer on layer.

'Fine,' I say. I try and make myself as small as possible. I imagine the lighter dissolving into my flesh, my ribs collapsing in on one other, and my heart shrivelling to the size of a raisin to be small enough to squeeze past.

I understand now, the reason the man smoked, not because it pleased him but because there is something gratifying in small acts of rebellion. It is sad that I did not think to thank him. When I reach my room, I retrieve the lighter from the vest and place it with the necklace in the pillowcase from under the bed. At night-time, I pull the pillow out. I sleep much better with the lumps.

The last time it happens, I am thirty-two.

The one I watch is small, not quite five foot five, yet looks strong. I like the combination. His hair is in the midst of growing out an ill-advised shaven head and it leaves him looking irritated. What would it feel like to run my hands over it? Would it scratch my palm? I almost feel it. It might be soft. Maybe the shave gave way to baby-hairs and it would be like to run a hand through the inside of a goose-feather duvet. I lean forward in my chair, I hope I might catch a scent. I can't. Instead, the smell of shitty coffee infiltrates my senses. I move my mug to the side of the table and try to ignore the fact the milk has begun to curdle at the top. I flinch when it clangs against the saucer.

The boy still doesn't look at me. I hate him a little for this. I want him to look at me. I want him to smile in the off-hand way that means nothing more than hello. I want acknowledgment. I want something from him. A gift. A gift that I can love just as he loves. Maybe the chain around his wrist, or the wallet from his pocket. Or the notebook wedged between the menu stand and his coffee.

I go to the counter and wait to order a drink. The line isn't long but the child in front lays at her mother's feet in protest. She laughs, as I snarl, and drags herself after her mother. I ignore the wave she offers.

I laugh with the barista as she jokes that men are over-grown toddlers that never order for themselves. I smile in my nicest *I know what you mean* way. I don't. She passes the order to a smaller girl who doesn't look me in the eye. One Americano. Table thirteen.

My bag and coat sit at the corner table and go to collect them. I take my time to push my arms through the sleeves. I leave my bag hanging off on shoulder with the buckle unclasped.

'One Americano for table thirteen!'

The spiky head twitches upwards but he doesn't move. He watches to see if anyone else steps up to take the drink but they don't. He moves his coffee to check his number. Thirteen. I'd already checked it twice.

'Table thirteen please'

He gives in, stumbles out of his chair, and his legs tangle with those of the table. His hands pull at the sleeves of his jumper and his cheeks burn. I take my moment and walk towards the exit past his table. I hear his voice speak to the barista and it almost stops me in its quality. It's gruff and guttural and everything I could have hoped for. I wonder what my name would sound like in that voice. Maybe I could love that voice. I can't stop however, as much as I'd like to. I nudge the notebook as I pass and it falls into my bag. I don't stop to look back. Not even when I hear the childish giggle that follows my departure.

When I arrive this time, my mother stands in my room. Her hand clutches an empty pillowcase and my treasures lie on the floor. I rush to her feet and scramble to get them all in my arms.

'What is all of this?' She asks. Her left foot twitches to prod a pair of earrings and I snatch them away.

'They're mine.' I say.

She stands still as I collect the last few things; the hair clips, the keyring, and the biro pen. I turn to her and wait for her to open the pillowcase before I pour them in and snatch it back. Her face twitches in the same way it always does when she wants to speak but can't find the words. She looks stupid. I nudge her towards the door with my elbow.

'When is dinner?' I ask.

'Ten minutes.' She says. She hovers but I don't acknowledge her. I place my pillow back on the bed, plumping it until the lumps lie right where I like them, before I lift my head. She doesn't meet my eyes, and instead focusses on my feet. No doubt inspecting the dirt that is smeared across the front. I almost take them off and throw them at her. At least then she'd have a job. I watch her focus flit for a split second and then she begins to turn. As always, she doesn't complete her task.

'I just wondered why that was in there.' She says it fast, almost to the point of it being incomprehensible. It takes me a second to understand what she's nods towards, but when I do I giggle.

'Well, why not?' My voice is two pitches higher than normal. My eyebrow rises in the way she hates but I love.

'Well, I just thought… That well you wouldn't want to have reminders around the house. That was what they said wasn't it?' She speaks more clearly this time. Her head is raised and she forces herself to meet my eyes. I give her one moment of victory before I reply.

'They were wrong. Of course, I want to remember. I loved him mother. Did you not love him?' I step forward. She leans back, desperate to not retaliate with her own step.

'No. No, he hurt you. Remember?' She shakes her head the way you would with a toddler. Exaggerated swings from side to side that borderline whiplash. I can't help but think that's the last memory she will have of being a mother. Telling me no. Always telling me no. Just like him.

'I don't know what you're talking about.' I collect the pillowcase once more and swing it in my right hand. It brushes against her knees.

'Yes, you do.' She breaks our eye contact and I've won.

'Mother, if I say I don't know then I don't know, do I?' The bag swings further now. It crashes into her with a jolt each time.

She looks up once more and I tilt my head and make my face imitate her own.

'Fine'

I choke a laugh down.

'Fine.'

'Dinner is in five minutes.' She says and paces out of the room.

Her footsteps grow distant as I add the newest gift to my collection. The notebook had been forgotten in my mother's interruption but now commanded attention. I place it in the pillowcase, mindful not to crush the glasses at the bottom. I sit the pillow on the bed and tuck it into the blankets. Nice and tight.

I turn to where her eyes landed. My dad's watch sits by the wall, the glass is cracked and the hands no longer move. Brown specs litter the face. The gold links have faded and it reminds me of the *cheap piece of crap* from my childhood. Melted down, I'm sure they would look indistinguishable. I bend to pick it up and walk towards the bed. I stop halfway and turn back around. It deserves an audience and so I find it a new place, on the dressing table just below my mirror. Its own stage.

When I go downstairs I smell charred metal and burnt water. It's dangerous to be alone at a certain age, accidents happen all the more often. Such a pity.

The ring fits perfectly on my finger. She would have wanted me to have it.

Zaid Hassan

ONE REBELLIOUS STRAND

I'm late. Probably only by a few minutes but still late. I didn't sleep in, didn't have to wait for the shower to heat up and didn't get stuck in traffic. I'm just late.

Timekeeping has never been a strength of mine. I just can't take time too seriously. If you ask me, it's just a neat trick to make us think life is always moving at the same pace. Truth is, life doesn't pass in seconds. Life moves at the pace of excitement. *Time flies when you're having fun* – why does no one mention that time drags when life's drab? I guess my lack of excitement ensured that time moved slowly this morning.

Figg's mouth hangs open and his spectacles seem to crawl down his nose.

'You are twelve minutes late and that is your excuse?' he asks in the lifeless tone reserved for call-centre managers.

I don't think he heard a word I said. That wasn't an excuse; that was an in-depth explanation. I flash a smile at him, then try and get my point across again.

'I see what you're saying, boss. I really do. But what I'm trying to say is that if nothing happened in the seven minutes that I missed, then I didn't actually miss anything and I'm not really late at all.'

Figg remains unmoved. His mouth opens but no words come forth, only a sigh and the thick aroma of stale coffee. He closes his mouth, pushes his glasses up his nose and walks away as if the conversation had never begun. Pretty much the reaction I expected. I'd experienced similar with my parents, my teachers, the police – basically any figure of authority I'd come across in my twenty-one years. I take a seat at my desk and begin answering calls.

Forty-five minutes in and I've resolved the issues of six customers. That should be enough to keep Figg happy for the time being. I wheel my chair back and look around to see if any of my co-workers aren't busy, but they are all buried in their little booths. The walls surrounding them are plastered with the same motivational posters that greeted me on my first day, except for one addition credited to myself. It was probably an immature idea but seeing 'WORK is a four-letter word' among phrases championing the value of teamwork and work ethic never fails to amuse me. I've always wondered why it hasn't been removed. In fairness, my poster is infinitely more fitting for a call centre than the one above it that reads, 'TEAM: Together Everyone Achieves More'.

I find nothing else to hold my attention and, to distract myself from the ceaseless sound of ringing phones, I plug in my earphones and play Pharrell Williams' *Freedom*. My fingers start clicking and I'm sure that if not for the earphones I'd hear myself humming along to the tune. Somehow, my body is now hot-stepping its way through the narrow walkway that separates desk from desk. A few heads are jerked away from their computers, but I pay them no mind. The movements I incorporate into my sudden dance include me removing a pack of Marlboro Golds from my pocket, raising it to my mouth, and extracting a cigarette using my teeth. I reach the lift and press the up button, still bouncing to the beat. The door opens, I spin inside and head to floor six.

When I open the door to the roof, fresh air rushes into the building. I fill my lungs as I remove my earphones. The first time I came up here I smoked sitting on the edge of the roof, legs dangling above seventy feet of air. As fun as that was, I decided to make other arrangements. Bringing a desk chair up here was easy enough, but there was one awkward moment when the elevator had stopped, without warning, at floor four. A group of middle-aged men in crease-free suits seemed rather disturbed at the sight of me sitting on a desk chair in the middle of the elevator. They didn't even get in, the doors slowly shut in front of them as their glaring eyes attempted to will me into non-existence. I guess they were going down. My chair hasn't moved from this rooftop since. I sit down and eventually spark up after battling the wind with my lighter. I watch the throngs of people bustling around the city centre as I smoke. I've never understood why the bodies seem so much more alive, more real, from this bird's eye view.

'You know that's killing you, right?'

I turn to see a well-dressed woman approaching, maybe thirty years old, holding a cup of coffee in each hand. Her dark hair is tied back neatly in a bun except for one rebellious strand swaying with the wind.

'Life's killing us, yet we keep on living, don't we?' I say.

She smiles, hands me a cup and, without asking if I'd mind or introducing herself, takes a seat on the ground next to me. I consider offering her the chair, but she looks comfortable, so instead, I nod and thank her for the coffee.

'They told me you were different,' she says after a pause.

I have no idea who this woman is or who *they* are, but I just smile back and sip my coffee.

I turn again towards the bustle of the city, my gaze flickering from one person to the next. She does the same, following my gaze, almost as if she's looking for whatever I might be seeing. There is tension in the air, but it's not uncomfortable. Her unexpected company is a pleasant diversion. I start to ask her a question, but she beats me to it and asks,

'Do you know who I am?'

She notices that we both attempted to break the silence at the same time and it makes her smile. I smile too.

'No, but I could venture a guess.'

She nods.

'You obviously work here, but you're not in my department... and you don't strike me as the type to share a coffee with a stranger on the roof.' I eye her pristinely white shirt. 'I'd say you're from HR and you've been sent to have a word with me."

'Sent? I'm not a parcel, I don't get *sent* anywhere.' There was no change in her expression or tone to match the indignation of her words. 'I was *asked* to review your performance and decide if you're an asset to the company or a liability,' she says, casually, as though we were still talking about cigarettes.

'Honest and straightforward,' I say. 'Not your average HR rep then. I wonder if *they* would say that you're different.' She raises her left eyebrow at me before I carry on, 'anyway, could you have refused?'

'Refused what?'

'Refused to review me.'

'Well, not without a legitimate reason, no.'

'So, you *were* sent, then.' I smile again as I say this, teeth showing this time.

She ponders this for a few seconds then shrugs. I assume she agrees with me. I take a few more drags on my cigarette, flick off the ash and watch as it disintegrates and gets absorbed by the gust of wind circling us. Everything is still below; even empty crisp packets and carrier bags are motionless. The wind seems to have adopted this rooftop as its home – as its shelter.

'What were you going to say, anyway?' she asks, regaining my attention.

'Sorry?'

'Earlier, when I asked if you know me, you were about to speak. What were you going to say?'

'Oh. I wanted to know how you managed to get up here with both your hands full.'

'Do you still want to know?'

'Not particularly,' I say. 'I suppose I was just making conversation.'

'No need for that, we already have plenty to talk about...', she pauses, tilting her head to one side and fixing her gaze on the distant grey skyline, '...it just doesn't yet feel like the right time to begin.'

'I agree. I was about to head out for lunch.'

She blinks and checks her watch.

'It's quarter past ten,' she says, looking up at me from under furrowed eyebrows.

I don't fancy going into the whole mechanics of time again, so I shrug, hold her gaze, and say, 'a man's gotta eat.'

'For three hours? So... Figg was not exaggerating about the lunch breaks. Your numbers were too high for us to take that report seriously, but I suppose we were wrong to dismiss him. Have you really been taking almost two extra hours... paid hours... for your lunch every day since you started? Where do you disappear off to? And how are you still exceeding your targets?'

I stay silent and keep eye contact for a few seconds before turning to face the city. I've never liked explaining myself and this question would, under normal circumstances, have been my cue to leave. I like this woman though. She's beautiful enough with her sparkling brown eyes but it's not a physical attraction I feel. The sparkle in her eyes spells mischief and I suppose that's why I stay and say, 'how about you continue your review over lunch and see first-hand?'

She blinks rapidly.

'That's not really appropr–'

'I'd like to set out some rules, though.' I cut her off because she's got the wrong impression. 'If you are to review me, then you should understand me. Observing me will not help in that sense. I reckon you'll need to join in and experience what I do before making your report.'

She snorts, then inhales deeply and asks, 'and what *do* you do?'

I shrug.

'I don't *plan* to do anything. I just catch whatever life sees fit to throw my way on any given day.'

Her whole body is now turned towards me and the wind has urged a few more strands of hair to escape her bun.

'You expect me to follow you blindly, then?'

'I don't expect anything from you, lady. It's your job to review me. Now, you could have called me up to your office or observed me while I worked, but instead, you're up here.' I gulp down the rest of the coffee and stub my cigarette in the cup. 'You can either go back to the office or wherever else you're sent and spend three hours that you'll likely forget by next week or you can come with me and maybe discover some of the secrets that this city holds. The choice is yours.'

She doesn't respond. I open my mouth to say more, then realise I have nothing to add. I stand and turn to leave.

'Do you give everybody this speech?' she calls out as I walk away.

I stop and turn to meet her eyes.

'Only those who have the time to listen.'

She holds my gaze for a long while before offering the slightest of nods. She stands, brushes the dust away from the back of her skirt, and follows me into my world.

Liam Heitmann-Rice

FOR THOSE WHO'VE COME

Kimberley got out of the car, locked it, and blew the hair out of her eyes. Sunshine slapped her skin with the shock of walking into a glass door. She was accustomed to the humidity in Hong Kong, but, even after twelve years in Australia, the summers here always felt tough and rubbery, like dry chewing gum.

Thirty-nine years old, five-foot-ten, usually dressed in black drainpipe trousers and a silk blouse, usually purple, Kimberley Cheung lived alone in South Perth. In lieu of children, she devoted her life to the Jade Palace Chinese Restaurant. She dropped the keys in her bag which was, as always, heavy. Two iPads, phone, charger, bottle of water, banana, bookings schedule, two diaries, and a packet of cigarettes.

Walking across the car park, Kimberley squeezed the back of her neck and told herself, 'Seventeen tables booked... Eight in the garden, nine in the Jade Room, and all the VIP tables. First arrivals, 6:30?' And then, in her mind, *Need to double-check. Not sure. Check the schedule.*

Kimberley's thoughts often overtook the speed with which she was able to process them. It was not unusual that her to-do list would update itself as she recited it aloud. She looked at her watch.

'Five forty-three.'

Kimberley continued to mutter to herself until she reached the Jade Palace. She glanced up at the large green banner suspended above the entrance. HAPPY AUSTRALIA DAY, it said in gold letters, with the same printed in Mandarin characters. Australia and China, unified in one banner.

This was the fourth Australia Day Kimberley had hosted at the Jade Palace. Even though she did not understand its appeal, she knew this holiday was always good for business. Australians loved to celebrate their country, which was the accepted way of saying they gorged themselves and got drunk. Her restaurant facilitated these activities.

Kimberley's friends would call today Invasion Day, but she ignored their implications. Australia's past did not interest her. She had come to this country for its present and built a business that gave her a riverside bungalow and a '17-plate Toyota. It did not weigh heavily upon Kimberley's conscience that this rendered her as self-interested as those who had colonised her adopted country two-hundred-and-thirty years ago.

She looked up at the banner once more and focused on AUSTRALIA, remembering a fragment of the national anthem she heard on the radio that morning:

> *For those who've come across the seas*
> *We've boundless plains to share.*

The automatic doors ushered her in like the hands of a master of ceremonies. Kimberley's cheeks tightened in the sudden coolness of the air-conditioning. Piano music fell from speakers in the ceiling like powdered sugar. Occupying the main body of the restaurant was the Jade Room, whose walls curved in one enormous circle. The tables were laid across the floor like canapés on a platter, while, on an elevated section of the room with floor-to-ceiling windows, a triplet of banquet tables overlooked the Swan River. Within weeks of opening, these tables had become regularly occupied by customers Kimberley referred to as The Money, whose arrival was declared as much by the loudness of their voices as by the strength of their perfumes. They were all cash, no culture – but they were profitable.

'Hi, boss,' Michelle said, looking up from a touchscreen monitor.

'Hi.' Kimberley dug the bottle of water out of her bag. 'It's so hot,' she drank, 'I can't believe it.'

Michelle laughed, 'It's nice and cool here, boss. Lovely breeze everywhere.'

'I'm so pleased.' Kimberley stuck out her tongue, and hoisted the bag further up her shoulder. 'This is killing me, so I'm going to throw it at something if I don't sit down soon. Tell me quick, how many tables reserved tonight?'

Michelle tapped the monitor, squinted, tapped again, and announced, 'Jade Room: ten tables, plus all three VIP tables. And seven in the garden.'

'Oh.'

'What's wrong?'

'Nothing.' Kimberley opened the bottle, drank. 'Got the reservations mixed up,' she said. 'Bye.'

'Bye, boss.'

Kimberley never asked to be called that, boss, but she did not consider it unsuitable. It was on her trial shift that Michelle had first said it, while being tested on the table numbers. Kimberley had corrected her and Michelle responded with, 'Okay, sorry, boss.' None of the staff had ever referred to Kimberley as anything other than Kimberley, and she would have found this insulting were it not for the respectful neutrality of Michelle's expression. She looked to Kimberley awaiting further instruction, not striving to antagonise, having simply called her 'boss' with no apparent awareness of the familiarity required for such an informal moniker. Kimberley accepted this as an invitation to the friendship that had since grown between them for almost two years. Both women were Asian by descent, although Michelle had enjoyed twenty-four years of Australian citizenship. The second-generation daughter of Chinese parents, she had lived in Perth her entire life but both Kimberley and Michelle shared the experience of being made to feel a foreigner in their own country.

Kimberley turned right into a corridor wallpapered with Chinese calligraphy and shouldered the kitchen door open. She passed the chefs, entered her office, dumped the bag on her desk and cried out in exhaustion as she fell into a chair.

Kimberley looked down again at her watch. 'Six twelve,' she told the empty room. The first reservations would be arriving soon.

*

A ripple of warm air touched Michelle's nose as the doors opened. A slim tanned woman strode in and ran her fingers through her hair, shadowed by a short, dark man in a white shirt. The woman's shoes were pointed at the toes, spiked at the heel, and red on the sole. The small logos on their clothing affirmed their wealth. Kimberley had told her about customers like this. It was very, very important that she be polite to them, even if they were rude, which they often were.

'Good evening,' Michelle said.

'Orright,' the man grunted.

'What's your name, please?'

'Elly Bleach,' the woman answered. 'We're booked on the big tables, right?'

'Of course, one moment.'

Michelle stared at the monitor, searching for their reservation. The man exhaled through his nose, watching her mouth out all the Sams and Deans and Bens, all those *Australian* names. None of this Xing Pi Ting Wong bullshit.

'Ah okay, yes,' Michelle said. 'Please follow me.'

Michelle led them up to the banquet table and stood aside as the woman folded herself into a chair, stiffened by the tightness of her dress. The man dropped to his chair like a sack of wet sand.

'I shall come back in a few minutes with some green tea for you both.'

'Nah nah,' the man said, 'bring us a wine list, would ya? Cheers.'

*

The Jade Palace Chinese Restaurant began as a derelict piece of real estate acquired in the early nineties by Kimberley's father. It was eventually christened the Cheung China House, and did not enjoy much success before foreclosing completely in the mid-2000s. As an only child, and with a much cleaner credit rating, responsibility fell upon Kimberley to redeem the property. She sold her apartment in Hong Kong and immigrated to Perth, when the death of her father left her an inheritance worthy of resurrecting the restaurant anew as the

Jade Palace. New furniture, new wallpaper, an extension overlooking the river, and new chefs who produced dishes that were reviewed in every national broadsheet from *The West Australian* to *The Sydney Morning Herald*. Some of these articles had portrayed Kimberley as an immigrant success story, a thousand words beside a photograph of her stood in front of the restaurant, staring confidently into the eye of the camera. A similar photograph of Kimberley's father was framed in her office.

She was standing by the front doors when Michelle came over. 'Boss, most of the reservations have arrived at the VIP tables. Just waiting on a few more people.'

'Good, that's fine. I'll go over and take a drinks order in a minute.'

A shot of laughter rang across the room. 'Sounds like they've had quite a few already,' Michelle said.

'They'll want more.' Kimberley watched one of the men standing at the banquet table swig a bottle of beer as he squeezed the behind of a woman beside him. 'They always do.'

*

The last of The Money had arrived.

'Oh my god, *hiiiiii!*' Elly's voice exploded across the restaurant as she leapt out of her chair.

Another tall, tanned woman called over, 'How you going, hun? Not seen ya in ages!'

They both wore short black dresses and impractical shoes. Both were blonde, their skin the same shade of bronze, and, as they embraced, the two women became one homogenous form. Even their voices were interchangeable, each word anonymised in a dialect of laughter and nonsense. One of them pointed to a bottle of Cristal and promptly upended it into two champagne flutes. Thin and golden, the glasses for a moment resembled the women holding them.

Kimberley strode across the Jade Room, ascended the steps, and placed her left hand on the shoulder of a man in a white shirt. 'Happy Australia Day,' she said, offering her other hand. The man turned around, looked at her face, down at her hand, shook it, nodded his head, and said thanks.

'How are all of you doing tonight?'

'Yeah, pretty good.' He sipped from his JD and coke. 'Ya'self?'

'Great, thanks! It's such a beautiful night. You should get a fantastic view of the fireworks from here.'

Kimberley looked through the window, across the river to South Perth. It was not a beautiful night; the sun was hours from setting and the sky was an acidic shade of blue. She returned to the man's face. It was hardened by sunburn, containing eyes that moved down Kimberley's straight black hair, to her lips, her small nose, and then to her own dark, almond-shaped eyes. He did not return the smile she offered to diffuse the hostile silence, instead folding his arms. Like his face, they were dark and covered in black hair. Kimberley supposed he was of Greek or Italian heritage, and she knew what these people were called in Australia. This man was a *wog*.

'Should be alright, I reckon. Look,' he said, 'can you get us some drinks?'

'Sure. What would you like?'

She had encountered men like this before, knew that they looked at her as a vending machine, a maid, an *Asian*. Men who believed this was their country, who sought to remind her with every curt sentence, and overlooked the fact their blood was as red as hers. But she welcomed them in with wide smiles and open arms, because they were The Money. Dignity was expensive, and these people handsomely remunerated her for abandoning it.

'We'll have a bottle of Malbec,' the man said.

'Of course.'

Kimberley walked to the bar and retrieved the bottle of wine, loading a tray with glasses. She blew the hair out of her eyes and returned to their table. Laid the tray down, uncorked the bottle in front of them all. Poured it into every glass, emptied it.

'Would you like another?' Kimberley asked.

The man nodded. Yes, they wanted more. More and more and more.

Kimberley presented them with a new bottle, wished them a good night, and said she'd be back later to see how they were doing. No-one paid attention. They had their drinks; everything else was irrelevant.

Kimberley decided to get something to eat from the kitchen, before it got too busy. It was going to be a long night and would only be lengthened by hunger.

She passed Michelle clearing plates off a table, who called out behind her, 'Boss.'

'Yes?'

'Happy Australia Day,' she said.

Kimberley shook her head and laughed. 'Isn't it just?'

Judith Howe

PROXIMITY

I refuse to romanticise him now,
To spit flower petals into his grave
I did not know the 19-year-old son, brother, friend, man.
Who I knew was the 11-year-old boy, but
he was just a boy
This poem is for the 11-year-old
All blue eyes, blonde hair, wide smile
Popular, but cried when my friend wouldn't date him
Big round pebbles of tears cascading as he asked me why over and over
Told me he loved her
With an earnestness only a child can produce, like
He couldn't imagine the sky without thinking about loving her.
I can't help turning him into an ideal eulogy when he wasn't an angel,
He was a little arrogant really,
Good looking, and knew it, but
He was an 11-year-old boy who for me never got any bigger than the day he cried.
He lived one road over from me for as long as I can remember,
And his childish face still hovers on my peripheral when I walk past his house
As I'm sure it does for his mother whenever she closes her eyes.
I expected to watch his life unfurl at a distance
Laugh at his bad decisions, bad tattoos, bad haircuts
Laugh at the idea of this being what that 11-year-old grew into
Smile at the kids I presumed he'd have one day
All that effervescent future just on the tip of his tongue, of everyone's,
But for him the bubbles fizzled into nothing
He wasn't a hero, or a martyr,
He wasn't even a great 11-year-old boy, but he was so familiar
Something I never expected to lose,
Thought I'd walk past on the street and watch him age, flick book style
His whole life, he lived one road over from me,
Just one road.

Becca Joyce

BETWEEN THE LINES

A DREAM

Running; always running. You don't know where you are but you can hear a piano playing somewhere and you are running. A heavy rain falls and there are strong winds tearing at your face, but you can't stop and you won't stop because you can't stop. There are footsteps behind, heavy and determined. Stomp. Stomp. Stomp. They never run. They don't have to.

Where are your shoes? You are barefoot in long grass. The long grass knots around you, and there's water on the grass, and there's water on your feet, except it isn't water. The water is red and the water is thick and the water isn't coming from the grass because it's coming from you. The footsteps are still behind. They always win. Stomp. Stomp. Splash. Footsteps in the red water. You can't get away. You can't look back. You can't move forwards. You try running; always running. Footsteps behind. Splash. Splash. Stop.

Silence.

You breathe slowly and you think you are free, but then a hand grabs the back of your neck. Thick, firm fingers press against your throat. The piano plays louder. You try to call out.

Silence.

You fall backwards into the grass where the water is red and you can see that the sky is red and your feet are red and your hands are red and there's red coming from your mouth and you can't breathe you won't breathe you can't breathe you–

SWEAT

You wake with a shout of silence, and a sour-saltiness in the thick air is stuffed down your throat; you choke against the pressure. An oppressive heat pushes against your naked flesh and you kick off the sheets that are tangled between your legs. Turning onto your back, you stare at the grey expanse of ceiling above you. You try to focus on controlling your breathing, but it runs away from you in short, sharp bursts and you pant into the dark.

Lying there in the dark, the Artex swirls that spread across your vision jut out towards you from above. The sharp shards pierce the air, and you can almost feel the sting of scratches as the points threaten to tear at your cheeks. You don't want to look at the ceiling anymore. As you adjust yourself into a seated position, the crumpled pillows behind you press deep into the small of your back, and your legs seem too long. Your toes push against wooden slats, the limits of your bed boxing you in and confining you to your thoughts. You're still having the nightmares, then.

You thought they'd stopped, but now you're not sure they ever will. You can't stop thinking about what happened, or what you did, or what you're still left to do. You can't stop thinking about her. There's so much to do, and you're so tired, and the nightmares ensure you never forget either of those things. Maybe one day, you tell yourself. There's a chance that one day you'll be able to close your eyes and see black instead of red, and you'll be able to sleep until night is over. One day. Maybe. Or perhaps the darkness just won't ever end.

After what feels like an age of lying trapped, you're finally able to fill your lungs without them screaming at you to stop. You relish the feeling, drinking in litres of cold air before daring to leave your bed. For some reason, you find yourself making your way to your desk at the other side of your room. You leave the bed, as usual, unmade behind you; a mess of knotted sheets and pillows thrown across the mattress with careless abandon. You clumsily drop yourself down into your chair, the short walk from dreams to desk draining you once more, and you reach across to flick on your lamp. You pause.

As your hand hesitates over the switch, you notice a strip of ripped skin by the side of your thumb and the blood underneath threatens to break through the surface. You press down on the switch and flood your desk with light, the blood of your thumb pulsing mockingly under the harsh, white glare. You screw up your hand into a fist and bring it down onto the desk. The resulting clatter of falling pens shreds through the silence of the night until the room becomes still once more. You take in another mouthful of cold air before expelling it harshly through your nose, and then you get to work.

A PHOTOGRAPH

Red lines. Red lines up and down. Thick, red poles from ceiling to floor, from front to back, from left to right. They're flecked with other colours, curling touches of yellows and greys and browns and blues where the paint has been chipped and scuffed and ruined. They're lots of colours, really, and yet it's impossible that they're anything but entirely bright red. It's aggressive and it's primal and it's alive. They bleed into the photograph, the red lines do. Veins, even. They bleed into the photograph and they bleed into the mind, and there they are. Up and down and left and right. They point here, they point there. They point this way and they point that, but ultimately they point to the body.

The red even bleeds into the floor. It's grey, for the most part. A shiny, speckled grey spreading out across the ground. It gleams under the cheap, bright light, throwing shards of white back into the air. The light bounces and melts simultaneously into the grey, swirling and fading and shining, and in the grey there is red. Tiny, red blemishes smudged into the floor, mixing with the grey and the white; a mottled mess of colour, with tiny, red blemishes dancing their way to the hideous blotch of the body.

Black squares. They race from the foreground to the back, shrinking as they go. A line of impenetrable, dark squares. They give the image the illusion of moving, running, falling. Those black squares, encased in frames of white, are reflecting the red lines. Red lines on black squares in white frames. 1, 2, 3. They lead backwards, where one other dense black square is sat screaming in the dead centre of the image. They lead backwards, pulling in to the depths of the photograph. Red lines on black squares in white frames, leading backwards to

THIRST

You're in your chair, the desk lamp angled towards a glossy A4 photograph in front of you. Your eyes skirt around the image for a while, focusing on the contrast of white paper on dark mahogany, but it's not long until you force yourself to look – to really look – at the body. Lying abandoned at the back of the underground carriage, clearly recognisable, is the pale and small and dead body of a young woman. She hadn't really lived yet, you think, and now she's dead.

No, not dead. That's not powerful enough. Killed. Murdered. Executed. Except none of these words seem right.

To put it quite simply, she was stopped.

You marvel at the way the photo frames the body so well. She lies in the doorway at the back of the carriage, red handrails perfectly squaring around her. The carriage number at the top of the doorway seems to title the scene. 92195. You think about how you will never forget that number, and how you will never forget this scene. You think about all the times you've travelled this route. You think about the thousands of people who have done the same. And then you think: why her?

The young woman is lying on her side. Her hair is unremarkable, a crop of brunette curls that frame her equally ordinary face, and she lays forgotten and anonymous. Her jacket has fallen open to reveal a white jumper. The jumper hugs her figure closely, wrapping itself around her waist, clinging on. The neck of the jumper is trimmed in black, and the contrasting line sits high against her collarbone. Not high enough, however, to cover up the thin, red mark that stretches around the young woman's throat.

You drag your gaze away from the discolouration and look at her face. Her young skin is imperfect; light freckles and acne scars adorning her forehead and her chin. Eyeshadow is smudged across the top of her nose, and there's a shimmer of the golden dust across the tops of her cheeks. An orange shade of lipstick, no doubt earlier carefully applied, is now crudely dragged across her mouth into a grimace. Her eyes are open.

The empty stare cuts right through you. Her eyes are brown, and they might once have been described as attractive, but now one of her pupils has blown to twice the size of the other. The asymmetry unsettles you. In her dark eyes you think you see the reflection of a figure, and it takes you a moment or two to realise that it is your own face looking back at you. You turn the photograph over and push yourself away from your desk, but you can still feel her watching you.

A REPORT

DATE: 06/07/17
CASE NUMBER: 17 8760 0748 A

REPORTING OFFICER: DI Rachel Yaxley

PREPARED BY: Constable Daniel Evans
INCIDENT: Homicide
DETAILS OF THE EVENT:
Police were dispatched in the West London area, arriving at Shepherd's Bush tube station at 0253hrs July 5th 2017, where they were directed by Transport for London staff to a held Central Line service. The as-of-yet unidentified body of a young woman had been discovered at the rear of carriage 92195 by TfL staff at approximately 0238hrs, when the police were promptly informed.

Cause of death is suspected to be strangulation by a single ligature; one visible abrasion is clear across the front of the throat. Currently waiting upon autopsy results to confirm.

Point of note: A matchbook advertising somewhere called 'Longwater' was found in the victim's pocket. No further identification nor any travel documents were found upon the body.

END REPORT

SCARS

Making your way downstairs comes naturally to you after countless nights spent in the sleepless search for relief, but the descent down the dark steps has reminded you of long, dropping escalators. You were searching for freedom, but you're instantly forced back to that night.

You can remember being in the carriage, but you remember very little else before that. A blur of artificial lights and rubber hand rails, and those long, dropping escalators that lead to dark, open holes. The carriage seemed longer than you thought they were. Rounder, too. The curved metal walls surrounded you completely, a metal sepulchre. Despite the suspended service, you're sure you can hear the echoes of trains in the distance. The dark beyond swallows unearthly winds, spitting out metallic screeches and an escalating thunder of machinery in return. Underneath it all is the gently played tune of a piano, an anonymous figure busking for their life. 'This is Shepherd's Bush. Alight here for...'

The memory ends. You come back to your senses at the bottom of your stairs, and you try to think of anything but the girl. You push open the door to your kitchen and survey the empty room. The blind, as usual, has only been pulled down two thirds of the way, and the dusky yellow glow of a street light floods across the bottom half of your cupboard doors. You glance down at yourself and observe the yellow strip that falls across the tops of your thighs, the murky light mottling against your blemished skin. Faint pink-purple lines scratch across the insides of your legs, hatching over a myriad of paler marks. The scars wrap around your thighs, and all you can see is the red-raw neck of the girl. You close your eyes tightly to fight it, but instead it prolongs the scene; the empty stare of her open eyes is branded onto the inside of your own.

Mari Lavelle-Hill

WINTER'S FOR FIDELITY

I held a bird in my hands with you
Your hands / over my hands / over wings
& your level voice / & the steep downs
Carving the ice off granny's bird bath
We are birds in the bath / toes and talons
Grasping perching birds / one toe in the bath
I'll be a bird / alone / in the vertical wood
Call me over / & I'll sing to you from the sill
This is why / I am always tapping at the window
This is why / my beak is yellow
This is why / my bones are hollow / my head too
We hold this bird together &
This is why / suddenly I am flying

Mari Lavelle-Hill

CHIAROSCURO

There's a recklessness in your sleep / never sound. [come dawn]
an anxiety between the brows / & your eyes no longer attend
the soft serve that these grumpy curves house. Perfunctory suits
you / kicks sweet in the knees / fits firm like your hand at my neck
[fuck this] feigned tossing / this isn't even a story / beer-cradled &
blue / I just wanted something to unwrap / to undo / to stop the
microwave's ding. [I'm done] in again / one hour gone / I leave
your stink up the sides of the bath / your dirty razor & its quills.
Love is just another word for / two toothbrushes by the sink. Sink in
slow / come hard / there seems to be a lot of strange commands
& I can't hear them all / through the fizz of my own [white noise]

Shannon Elizabeth Lewis

THE WORLD ACCORDING TO K

'Yes, that's me.'
There were officials at the door. The one with the big nose handed K several stapled pieces of paper.
'Wait... isn't this that literature survey thing?'
K recognized the loopy handwriting. Big Nose nodded.
'We had hundreds of thousands of applicants. You won.'
K leaned against the doorframe.
'No shit.'
Lettuce-Between-Teeth cowered, reverent.
'So, what did I win?'

*

'Hello! Welcome to Phase 6 of the Utopia Creation Project. We have spent years compiling questions on topics ranging from religion to artistry; it's now your job to sift through them. All answers must be given in 'yes'-or-'no' format. Once an answer is recorded, it will become *the* answer. All 207 localities of the UCP are in agreement. Do you understand?'
K tapped the desk.
'You mean, whatever I answer is the be-all-end-all answer for eternity? And everyone's just gonna believe it?'
The suits turned to look at Dry Skin.
'Yes. Note how I have given an answer in a 'yes'-or-'no' format.'
'What if I don't know?'
There was silence.
'We must give answers in a "yes" or "no" format.'
'Thought that was *my* job.'
Huge Pores whispered to Dry Skin.
'We are leading by example.'
'Why me?'
Dry Skin pulled out another index card.

'This organization was founded on the basis that all governmental, ideological, and otherwise dogmatic systems have failed. Conflict, war, terror. The UCP thinks it possible to abolish these. We had our experts compile questions about the most important literary and artistic pieces regarding radical structures – *1984, Brave New World, The Time of the Hero,* Banksy – and sent out a survey. Only citizens well-versed in these monumental works made the final selection. Then we randomly chose one individual from that list. You. Now... ready to begin?'

K leaned back.

'Yes.'

'Good. Easy ones first, then specifics. Government?'

Pen-points hovered, the potential for a thousand happy years waiting in their ink.

'Yes.'

Scribblings of the future filled the air.

'Crime?'

'No.'

'God?'

'Excuse me?'

'If the question is unclear, I can rephrase it. Is there a God?'

'H-how am I supposed to know that?'

'Please phrase your question in a–'

'Yes... yes... I know.' K sat forward. 'I guess... I was raised Jewish... but I never went for all that fire-and-brimstone stuff, you know? Then, I can't say definitely no. I don't know that. There must be a reason so many people believe. What if I say yes?'

Dry Skin gestured at a sizeable pile of papers.

'We go into specifics later.'

'All that just about God?'

'Yes... well, encompassing all known and practiced religions.'

'Oh... what if I don't subscribe to any of those?'

'Perfectly acceptable.' Dry Skin pointed to a pile of papers twice the size of the previous, 'We've accounted for that.'

'Well shit... this isn't gonna be an in-and-out activity, is it? What if I say no?'

'We move on to a question about economics.'

K stared at the papers. There must be at least fifty pages in the smallest pile. The print was miniscule. Eyebrow flipped through a couple pages in the larger pile. They were double-sided.

'No. I'm gonna go with no.'

There was a pause. For the first time, the suits felt the power of K. K's glory. Dry Skin and Eyebrow shared a look.

'The free market?'

*

The Process was undertaken over what is now called Glorious Week. K was provided with all necessities. They wanted K to be comfortable, in peak condition. Lunch included a side dish of spinach and a chocolate bar.

The results were fed into the Great Computer. K was transported to New Capital, an island on the Equator. The Week of Greater Glory ensued. Peace settled where UCP stood. Twelve new locations enlisted. K ruled with unprecedented grace.

Then the week ended. Unsavory characters of incorrect opinion began popping up. The UCP had expected this. What ultimately surprised them were the opinions. People were not initially disgruntled about politics nor non-God. The first official group of deviants bonded over K's decision to ban disco. They were sent off in UCP-brand-ABBA-and-Beegees-bearing rocket ships. Truth belongs here; deviants can roam the galaxy in search of their future.

Next went the communists, disappointed their ideals had not come to fruition. They spent weeks working around K's commandments, but truth comes with no compromise. They were shot into the stars in a bright red rocket. Holocaust apologists, corrupt city planners, gynecologists with cold hands, they all found themselves in rockets over the ensuing months. K was at every takeoff, wishing farewells and congratulations.

The expulsions were peaceful, aside from one group of gun-lovers who broke into a UCP office and demanded the right to weaponize. There were twenty people there at the time. Terrified, they phoned K, who appeared immediately. K entered alone, shining. All twenty survived, and the gun-nuts emerged in such a state of rapture that they willingly burnt their weapons before boarding rockets. K gave a speech that day. I learned every word.

Daily, deviants undertook their noble exile. Criminals, neo-Nazis, art critics. We were free, finally, of their poison. I burned for New Capital. Soon, I was prepared for the move. It was around then my own parents had to go. They were cat people, though K had been clear on this being a dog-loving paradise. I forgave them – K commands forgiveness – and watched them disappear into the clouds.

I have been in New Capital for a year. It is like nothing I could have dreamed of. Near K, few survive more than six months before they sow the seeds of deviancy. The streets lie empty. Three weeks ago, K found me. I have not left K's since. It is a holy place.

It is just me and K here. The prodigious offspring of the UCP. K tells me stories about the past, about horror and fear, about the present and peace. My heart races. K is beautiful. I am beautiful. This world according to K, purged of its aches and pains, it is heart-wrenchingly beautiful.

Jaime Lock

KITCHEN SCENES

I watch her making eggs in the kitchen and I watch him sitting at the table scrolling through his phone eyeballing those he barely knows she's invited him over – wanted to treat him to a nice breakfast – wanted him to know she cares enough to make him breakfast – hasn't seen him in a while but they aren't really speaking much just a few words hitting the dust and when the toast pops his head stays glued to his phone, thumb scrolling past the screen faces watching all the screen places filling all the blank spaces in the air with knee bounces under the table and she brings his breakfast over and he looks at the space between her eyes and tells her thanks and he chews it with his mouth open like a child or a dog 'the eggs would have been better if you added milk when you scrambled them' it's hard to say if she cares but she looks away instead of into his eyes maybe she knows she'd see hardness and anyway he's busy looking at the screen faces watching all the screen places filling the blank spaces in the air with knee bounces under the table and it reminds me of all the kitchen scenes I realised were wrong at thirteen the routine where my mum would do the cooking as well as the washing up after a full day at work and I feel my hands get clammy as I watch my best friend now at twenty slipping down the hole my mum can't find the energy to scramble her way out of so she just puts his food on the table moves to the living room and scrolls past screen faces watches all the screen places fills all the blank spaces in the air with television programmes and pets and forgets that she doesn't deserve anything less than devotion.

Jaime Lock

RING

The ring sits on her finger more gracefully than she thinks
mine hangs from my nose
like a cow, she told me she felt like tying string around it –
I couldn't help wondering where she would lead me, in bed

once I gave her the ring I made from a rod of silver
I soldered it then I battered it with a hammer to make a dappled effect but
mostly I battered it to mask that it wasn't straight

By mistake, a child bites her finger instead of just eating the hula hoop
from it.
When I was a kid, I had husbands until I was hungry
or until the gelatine would sweat in the summer heat and
I'd eat my ring

fast like we ate the party rings that time when you broke your diet
(I miss when)
you'd ring me five times and still have loads to say
when things were still being picked like blackberries and
when all these rings meant as much as the wedding one.

Jaime Lock

ON GASSING PIGS

My dad told me its eyes were too person-like,
eerily smart and like it knew
                      what was coming.
The last sow was sold, she remembered
the face that tugged her children from her nipples and
like any mother
                                    she went for it.
Full blown heavy weight force
under the free-range sky,
            knocking over the knee that buckled
yesterday under her back scratch.   I'll use you as a
tree trunk to itch myself against and you'll slap my side

        and call me good girl.

My dad told me the human
food makes her body sweet and besides, they can't get enough!
Hear them screech at the sight of cake
                    like it's all they live for –
skin extra tasty crunch crackling on the plate   eat me
on a first date, just don't think too much
about

the eyes that watch the trailer
           returning empty down the muddy path,   or

the three of us it takes to angle   the barricades
so the pig can't see the ramp it trotters up
or the lowering
        into
                the
                      stunning
or the up-to-30-seconds before.

Adam Maric-Cleaver

WHEN SHALL WE HEAR FROM LOBSTER?

(OR THE STORY OF THE FASCINATING MAN)

Lobster hasn't been heard from. That is not unusual. He throws a stone into a lake but we don't hear about it. He might be doing anything. He is almost certainly dead, having lived in the distant past. But he might be throwing a stone.

The stone breaks the surface of the water. It might not do, but our understanding of stones and water would suggest this is the only outcome. Our understanding of Lobster is sketchy. Reverend Stokes tells me, frequently, in the cheaply carpeted church study, that he believes that Lobster is not Lobster's real name. He is convinced that Lobster's real name is Crab.

'It is the only thing that makes sense. You see, I knew a man named Crab.'
'Was he Lobster?'
'No he was Crab. But Lobster's name might be Crab. Do you understand?'
'I hope I do. You might be the wisest man I know.'

But the wisest man I know is Lobster, the man who is not heard from and might or might not throw stones. I have devoted my life to studying him along with the Reverend Stokes, my teacher in all this. And today I have made a breakthrough. But first, one must understand Lobster.

His stone throwing is legendary in our town, which looks exactly like how one would expect a town to look. It looked exactly how I expected it to look and how Lobster expected it to look.

The legend about the stone throwing says that Lobster came here whilst there was still a lake in the centre of the town. Allegedly the lake had either green or brown plants around it, depending on the season. Nobody knows what season it was when Lobster came to our town.

So Lobster seeing the lake and, being legendary for his stone throwing skills, began throwing stones into it. He was wearing either a cravat, a dress shirt, a dress, pantaloons, a primitive form of denim, a badge, a crest, a bowler hat, a top hat, stilts or a leather tunic. He might have worn any number of these things in any combination though, as Reverend Stokes often says to me, it would have been unwise to wear the cravat in combination with the leather tunic, as, regardless of colour, leather is aesthetically toxic to ties. And, I add myself, leather sleeves are not ideal for throwing stones.

For Lobster did throw the stones. He did not skip them. He simply threw them and let them sink down. All the 'townsfolk', as the town's people were known at the time, came to watch him throw the stones, the ballet of rising and sinking.

Each stone seemed to penetrate the lake at a jaunty, novel angle. The splashes never gave the impression of randomness, but rather of sculptures pushed up, unwillingly and forcefully, from some reserve of beauty that the lake had hitherto not outwardly displayed, but always possessed.

Eventually, after a solid week of throwing, the water of the lake had become completely displaced and formed a moat around a pile of stones. Lobster was up to his waist in water. He stopped throwing stones and climbed out of the moat. He then decree that a town hall should be built on the mound of stones. He was told The Town Hall was on Bleecher's Street around ten streets away.

'Not *The* Town Hall. *A* town hall.'

There was a hum of acknowledgement. Everyone was terribly impressed.

'What is your name?' asked someone, wondrous.

'Lobster,' he said magnanimously, deeply.

This is all. A town hall stands, completely empty, on the lake to this day.

The Reverend Stokes and I were not present at the stone throwing but we have heard about it from some of the younger citizens of the town, the only people still gullible enough to believe such an obvious falsehood and wise enough to see that it was all true. For there was a Lobster, that much I am convinced of, if only for one detail in the legend.

Lobster promised to write, to the whole town. This was a terrible mistake on the part of Lobster. For one thing, the post office in our town is famously disorganised and cynical. Any unusual name, to or from, on an envelope is immediately discarded, if it is ever found at all.

For another thing, our town never forgets. And thus, in spite of nobody but the young believing the legend, we still await Lobster's correspondence eagerly. Lobster was probably just being polite. He had no intention of communicating, by letter or any other medium.

Such a useless piece of mythic shrapnel, a promise that could accountably disprove the myth with its very absence, was a sure sign that everything about the legend was true. The creator of the legend (who does not exist because the legend is true) could have very easily left his tracks covered by just saying that Lobster went away, saying nothing, vowing (maybe) never to return. But no. There was a reference to a correspondence that never comes. It was all the evidence I and Reverend Stokes needed.

(A town hall standing on a bed of stones is not evidence of any kind. It had been there longer than anyone could remember. There may never have been a lake, only a moat. No centre, only a rim.)

Reverend Stokes is truly a great teacher to me. Not in religion, you understand, for I have no interest thereof. Rather, he is the leading authority on Lobster and his legend. He has written one heavy tome interpreting multiple versions of the myth from multiple perspectives, scanning for inconsistency, probing for Marxist undertones, digging for individualist epigrams and mining (and this most importantly) for bullshit.

'Bullshit,' he often says to me, looking in the glare of the light bulb above his desk, 'Bullshit is the key to all great civilisations. And that is what this town is: a civilisation unto itself, born from a legend as the Sky Woman birthed man in the Iroquois creation myth.'

Reverend Stokes' book on Lobster is filled with such frivolous references to Native American creation myths. It is the only other field he has any true interest in.

The book is called 'A Stone's Throw: How Far Are We From Knowing Lobster (or Crab As I Call Him)?'.

It has been read many times by both myself and Reverend Stokes, and we both agree that it is a marvellous piece of scholarship.

'To think,' the Reverend intones, when I mention the book at his behest, 'that without Lobster, or Crab as I call him, so much would not be. My book would not exist, for instance. Our friendship, not undone, but never 'done-up' in the first place. Society; doomed. We are held together by our stories, you see.'

'Even if,' I add, 'those stories go absolutely nowhere.'

'Precisely.'

'Even if they can only suppose at a truth, be neither here nor there, but know that both here or there exist.'

'Indeed.'

'And even if, as in this case, the story influences the town in no discernible way other than by its very existence, as opposed to having legitimate content.'

At this, Reverend Stokes flies into a rage. The trusted rock of my life, of my bare bones existence, sustained only by the hunt for Lobster and Reverend Stokes' companionship for five whole years, now berates me for a pinhead, orders me out of the church study and into the street.

The reason for my rebellion is the breakthrough I have made today. You see, a letter was delivered to my house only this morning, in a brown envelope. It did not have my address on it and I am inclined to believe that the window blew it in, as there was certainly no chance anyone had been outside my door.

The envelope said 'From Lobster'.

I was, you can be sure, intrigued. For whilst most of the town do not believe the legend of Lobster, all wonder when they shall here from him. This is what I meant by my last comment to Reverend Stokes, my now former friend, the comment that I was yet to make when I read the letter.

I opened the envelope. There was a letter inside. This is what I had expected from my understanding of envelopes, but one must never suppose such things too strongly.

I read the letter. During the reading of the letter I was unsure what I felt. I shifted between happiness, dismay, boredom even and myriad of sensations that I'm sure you can imagine.

Here is what the letter said:

Dear Townsfolk

I must say that I do not remember your name, nor the name of any town I pass through. For all I know, your town has no name. I don't know the gender of the person who shall read this. In fact I do. No one shall read this.
I promised to write and I have, although I have taken measures to ensure that this letter will never reach you and never be read. I do not send these letters, merely place them in a large pile next to my desk.
Outside my room or shack or clearing, for it is always changing, there is always a hungry dog. I feed him the letters I have written at a rate of ten letters per day. There is not chance that any of you will ever read this letter or any of the others.
I could tell you where I am, perhaps what I am wearing, how I have changed since I walked through your town. I could be honest. This letter will not be read, so I could be truly, truly honest.
I will not do this. I don't wish to disappoint my fans, who I assume exist, although I do not know what they do. Once they hear of what I am doing, what I am wearing, I shall be reduced in their eyes and I cannot bare this. I would not know how to describe it. I shy away from simile and metaphor. They make it all so real.

Anyhow, please write back soon.

Lobster

I walk through the streets of my town thinking about the letter. There are many different buildings, all of them identical. I wonder what Lobster is smelling right now. Is it similar to I am smelling? Is the world he sees similar to the one I see? Where can the join be formed if not through contact?

'How Far Are We From Knowing Lobster?' asks Reverend Stokes' book.

My overall feeling is that of disappointment. I might never know if Lobster is throwing stones at *this very moment.* I reach the moat that surrounds a town hall.

I can tell you that my studies were long and vigorous and now seemed perfectly wasted. Our whole town, our little civilisation, is formed on a man who could be doing absolutely anything right now, who could be doing anything and even knowing he is there does not allow us to progress.

I wade into the moat a little, for it is a hot day. I no longer know what is even interesting about Lobster, other than the people he left behind, who I have not truly mentioned here (aside from myself and Reverend Stokes). They probably mean as little to Lobster as he means to them, and as much.

The sun is out. It shines like a probing eye, curious. I am perplexed, disappointed and at peace.

At peace with the fact that, even with the letter, I am just one member of our humble town still asking themselves:

'When shall we hear from Lobster?'

Lucy May

GADD.

The crackle
fills up my senses, a voice
sings to me
across the ribbons. A man in a cassette,
A man in song, a man
of handpainted landscapes, who am I to question
the key ingredient, a man of
handpainted blue, a man I'll never hear except through this crackle, this
birdwatcher, this dusty tang of wood smoke, these four wooden sides that
open out into
handpainted
red-breasted
blue-crested
flight across the years, this man who is the picture on the wall, this man
who is a song
filling up my senses, a man who is still
swinging,
mid-motion,
through all nineteen years of me to shatter the frame,
club and handle, all mine and I never even laid my eyes
upon smiling green under crackling autumn skies, leaves
twirling down to greet them and their melted run-on of stories all bleeding
together all
steadtler ink and strings this man,
this glorious brushstroke, this hummingbird-heart, this man
who I can never have, this man
who brings a tear to my eye this man who is
my mother, this man in the cassette, this man who is
hers.

Lucy May

STAINLESS

I was never allowed to touch the stainless-steel kettle, it was always too hot. I learned to make tea in an electric but the scream of soldier-blue still scalds. Those small cottage-windows, MDF scar tissue still there from where he climbed through. Crooked teeth and blind as the colour of the sky on those rainy afternoons, summertime mud and buzz all the way up to our house, all over the Christmas-Eve sofa, that stainless cream-puff sofa. We once left some chocolate on there by accident, so we turned over the cushion to hide the mess but he found it, he found the stain anyway, in less than five minutes. Didn't even have to see it, a sixth sense for stains.

He used to take us to watch the kites, bitted loose like the sky had been ripped away to reveal the colours, a shredded sunset on Bolehill where he can still point to each house, every home and who lived there, and on the hillside it looks like a mosaic of slate roofs and old Beatles records from the garage that were still intact even though the cardboard was damp, every single one. She took the picture-disc up to her room and refused to play it, refuses to play it, the brightness not faded on any of those four moustaches because she's so afraid to ruin them singing in the sky with diamonds or under the sea, she only wants them bright inside her ears like the spin and crackle of the record stores still swelling in the pipes of my ears, making grey skies marble and stop.

The same songs play through a bedroom window. She's probably listening to them now, walking home, up the inhale-exhale of those paving slabs with the trees nodding blossom in the springtime, cascading dewy tears over the shoulders of the street. Spine so jagged she has to savour it, that ancient dip built onto in the slick lines of the arts tower and those hideous diamonds they put over the hospital. Empty factory faces, grotesque. A steel strung heart all wired and wound tuneless, out of shape, bound up and knitted together like my eyebrows when I think of it and its borderlines that blur into one repeated mesh of city and sky and city and sky and city and sky and you pause

to breathe in the green.

Lucy May

WEDNESDAY'S CHILD

Undo me into mornings. Crisp and bright
      on weekends stretching out along the view,
      or in windows flickering on at night.
I'll be the trees unwinding arms for you,   ferns
              unpeel their eyes and watch us follow
        the silent sounds of running water.
Let me lie down in the street and swallow   myself back, I've been
sister, girlfriend, monster, doll, a daughter
unstitched to find the holes, colander heart, wandering parts, may I
ask for another page
of
paper weights for all the notes I've spun
      and hung above my bed to drip and dry,
           the words come unwritten before my eyes, they're coming
           undone.

Jono McDermott

WAITING FOR THE NEXT BUS AT THE CORNER OF OLD RD

Cigarette smoke. Nipping my eyes and clogging my nostrils. Sunburn through the shelter. Need a scarf to guard my nostrils. Didn't bring one because of the sun. I'm retired but I'm still not prepared for everything. Makes me wonder what life's all about, really.

Quick glance at the chap who's breathing out the filthy fumes. There's two of them. Oh God! no, that one's a girl. The fashions these days. I can't help staring a little too long, taking in the short, spiky, grass-green hair, the silver-crusted ears, the veins of ink encasing her arms, the ripped jeans. Watch as her equally-tattered companion reaches his hand up to his mouth, nimbly passes a bland brown stick through his lips, waits a second and reclaims it, letting a billow of fresh foulness flare into the empty air, like warm breath in winter – an entire world separate from the salty summer crawling over my tired skin. What pleasure could one ever gain from inhaling that poison?

The girl's glance snaps up to meet mine.

Smile? Look away? Heart's a timid little bird in a brittle bone cage. She wouldn't hurt me, would she? Clutching my bags too tight: nails digging into my palms. Feels I've skirted danger my whole life, oh please don't let it all end here!

She smiles.

I smile. Grip loosens on the plastic handles. I feel the lines my nails have left.

Maybe I shouldn't have judged her like that, lovely lassie that she probably is.

Phew! Another lungful: I let my guard down. I can't stop myself from coughing. I don't want to offend them, but I'm choking. Oh God! I can't stop now. Where's my tissue? I've got one up my sleeve, oh! where is it? where is it? There it is. My bags clatter to the ground beside me. Trying to smother my coughs in the tissue.

'You all right?'

Make an effort to nod. I'm not helpless! I'm just choking on your friend's stupid smoke!

There's a gentle pat on my back. A great cough heaves itself out and I'm okay again. I look up. Little Miss Green-and-Spiky's standing right beside me, the strong musk of roses rolling over me. She's clearly concerned. Bless her! It hardly seems to matter why I needed her help in the first place.

My gratitude stumbles out of my mouth in an unforced 'Thank you!'

'That's all right.' Her eyes are still caring for me. Her eyes, my goodness! There's more paint there than in the Galerie de Rêve. She stoops, saying: 'Here, I'll get your bags for you.'

What chivalry! An unbidden, insincere protest leaps out of my mouth. She continues replacing my shopping, tins at the bottom, groceries at the top, the way I stack it too.

Oh, how badly I misjudged her! My guilt pushes out more gushes of gratitude, until I see she doesn't need any of it. Glance up to where she and her friend were standing. He's gone now. Good riddance. Though I shouldn't –

'What bus are you waiting on?'

Bus. Takes me a moment to change the subject in my mind. Bus? The answer suddenly bounces out: 'The 27.'

'Ah, me too! Where you headed?'

'Home.' Obviously. Duh! She meant which street. 'Aerop Lane.'

'No way!'

Hmm? What does she mean? Oh! she means –

'That's where I live too! I've just moved in.'

How lovely, to know I live on the same street as such a kind-hearted young woman. I remember a certain house For Sale. A little plummet takes place in my stomach. Oh dear. Youths can be rowdy. I have to know. 'Number seventeen, is it?'

'Yes!'

The plummet redoubles.

'Are you nearby?'

Am I nearby? 'Yes. I'm in number fourteen.'

'Ah! Right opposite! Wow! that's uncanny.' Her delight seems really genuine. How lovely! She shifts the shopping bags she's still holding into one hand, and holds out her free hand to shake mine (a handshake between women!) 'I'm Lauren.'

Oh! the awkward obligation to introduce myself. 'Elizabeth.' Sounds so plain and raw in the still suburban air. I present my hand. Hers is soft and warm; mine – I become suddenly aware – rough and cold. More like a man's hand. What a first impression. Handshakes say a lot. Her grip is strong – not tight, but confident – she leads the handshake.

'Elizabeth? Nice to meet you!' Impeccable manners.

*

Heart's a happy little bird, proudly circling in its nest. Hands are shaking a bit. From excitement or unsteadiness. I don't know. Light wafts of rich chocolate tickle the back of my throat. Glance down at the tray. Oh, they're marvellous!

She'll love them. Young folk can't resist sweet things!

Look both ways. Strain my ears through my aid. One car coming from the right. I wait. Watch. Oh, it's going away to the right. Duh! Step onto the road. Remember to check the other way! No, still nothing coming. Over I go then.
Her house still looks overgrown. Bushes and flowers are sneaking into the street, rhododendrons peeking next door and through the windows, garden grass learning meadow ways. Wonder how long it'll be before she gets the mower out? Maybe I could offer my services, do a bit of gardening. A little chuckle of a laugh rattles out of my throat – as if I could really be of any use to her! But I'll offer anyway. Who knows what could happen?

Rusty little gate. Now where's the latch? How do I open it with both hands holding the tray? Approach side-on. Try and push it with my foot. Nope. Peer over the top. Where's the latch? Ah, there! Oh, it's not a latch, I just need to… lift it. Oh dear. How on earth am I supposed to do this? Step back. Can't risk the tray bakes. Set them down somewhere? I look around. Wall? Sloping. Ground? Unhygienic. Bushes, lamppost, postbox – postbox? Too far away. Can't leave a tray of home bakes lying on a postbox in the middle of the street. A kiddie or a cat or something might come along and steal them, or knock them over. My eyes drop back down to the wall. Balance one end of the tray on the wall? Risky. I step back over to the gate and carefully rest one end of the tray on the wall. I take away my right hand, slowly. Heart's tiptoeing now. Keep eyes on the tray. Grope for the gate. Metal touches my fingertips. There it is. Fingers grip an unfeeling metal bar. Lift. And push open! My right hand automatically whisks back to the tray. Steady.

Feeling a bit exhausted now. But triumphant. After opening a gate! Sun's baking my back. This summer's making itself known, all right. The rest of the walk up to her door is over before I've noticed I'm walking. Her door stands under a stone archway. Hanging baskets on either side, trailing dead vines, spindly webs. Suddenly the summer inferno is doused. Goose-pimples swarm up my arms and legs and down my back. Wow! it's cold in the shade. Hurry up and get inside. It'll be warm in her house. Time to knock on her door. The tray. Oh dear. Look around her door. No bell. No knocker. Letterbox is at ground level. How to do this? I could shout. What would I shout? *Hello? Lauren? I've brought you over some tray bakes!* Cheeks flush with preemptive embarrassment. Couldn't do that!

Okay. What can I do? Can't knock, can't ring, can't shout. *Could* knock. But where to put the tray? Glance around. Boxes. Aha! Cardboard boxes! Of course. She's just moved in. Hope they're firm enough. Give it a little try. Shuffle over to the boxes. Carefully set down the tray. Judge the support. The door's close enough, I only need to let go with one hand. Right, let… go… Quickly lift hand to the door. There's no door there, there's a person.

'Oh, hello, ah… Elizabeth?'

Yikes! I jump, drop the tray, stagger back, heart's trying to fly for its life!

Words flutter out after it. I don't hear them. Brain keeps falling, thoughts can't catch the world.

'Oh, God! I'm sorry! Are you all right?' My arm's clutched.

Vision levels out. The damp summer shade starts to dry up into a pleasant rosy perfume. I look around, into a pair of oil painting eyes, peering kindly down at me. The spiky-haired girl from the bus stop. Her name's Lauren, for goodness sake!

'Oh! my dear, you gave me a fright!' Who did I think it was anyway? The grim reaper? What am I like? jumping like a jack-in-the-box!

'Sorry! Are you all right?'

'Yes! yes! I'm fine.' Reflex answer. Legs ignoring gravity, heart flapping its wings apart and lungs cooking curry. Hardly fine.

'I, uh... D'you want to come in? Wow, did you make these?' Her words sprint from one ear to the other, poor old brain's like a cartoon cop, can't catch a thing. 'They look really nice. Right, d'you want to just...'

Pressure on my arm. I follow her into her house.

'That's it. Mind the step. Right, just through here...'

Air's not stale. No bitter nose-hair singe. Fresh. Draught brushing my cheeks. Wasn't it empty for years? Can't have been. Smells better than mine. How's she managed that?

Spacious place, far bigger than mine. Walls crumbling. Bricks showing. No wallpaper. Needs a vacuum. What's the living room going to be like? Will she give me tea? Wait! where are my tray bakes?

'Don't worry, I've got them here.'

I said that out loud. Through a doorway. Into a cavernous space, carved marble roof-beams a hundred feet in the sky, colourful painted ceiling stretching into the distance, freckled with bright little lights, lush trees bursting forth from a fuzzy floor like lampposts lining the road.

'They look amazing!'

Amazing. Amazing. Incredible. Move my eyes around the sight before me. Gorgeous, gilded paintings and swirling screens adorn the walls. Vines escort the glowing wires from place to place. Weird, unnatural statues stand here and there. Fancy glass staircase curves down to the floor. Like Hollywood colonised by Chichén Itzá.

Suddenly aware of the girl again. This is her house. How can this – ? Impossible. This isn't a house. Turn 'round. Look through the doorway, the dilapidated hall. So normal. The world I left behind. Want to go back! Back! Back!

Glance around at her. Standing beside me, holding the tray bakes. Looks embarrassed. Glance back at the giant room. Too big. Too big. But beautiful. Impossible. Beautiful. 'How is this – ?'

'This is my home.'

'Who are you?'

She tells me. I relax. I turn back to the room. I smile.

Ellie Meikle

COLLECTION OF POETRY BY ELLIE MEIKLE

THE WREN

    And I heard her crying into her sons' hugs
    in the yellow kitchen, saying
    how small she is, how like a wren she is,
    how her hand is smaller without
    another hand to hold it,
    and later, I see a wren in the garden,
    brave and round and small as a golf ball,
    beautiful, eating the seed left for her
    by the other wren, who occupies the house,
    she has a spine so strong you can feel it
    through her raincoat when we hug goodbye at the station,
    when she sends me kisses over the barrier

MY DAD

    My dad weeps so easily it's like turning a tap,
    plucking a flower, like watching a frog
    leap out of your hands
    he has studied philosophy and artificial intelligence,
    My dad can fix any virus your computer
    might ingest, he stores
    things up like them too, he says
    reality is sadder than Tom Waits,
    and when he plays Rain Dogs in the car
    I ask him not to put on another whole
    album that sounds like depression
    warmed up and grew teeth
    My dad is the most brilliant man
    he has studied John Locke and electric sheep
    at university, he says
    you are much more together than I was at your

age, he says you know a great deal
about how you are feeling
and I don't know how to correct him,
because he's the most brilliant
man

SHIRT

She brought his old clothes
and we tried them on,
so we could reuse them,
so we could wear the smell of him,
and I would not wash his shirt,
I wore it again and again, remembering him
at the piano, him laughing,
refusing to wash out the smell
of his body, refusing
to let that body depart forever
strange, that the shirt should outlive him
and like a hallucination,
the smell remained,
like a blessing, he clings to me,
he refuses to be forgotten,
refuses to be only a shirt and not a man

Catherine Mellor

THE FOURTH WALL

Carl woke to beating wings and Ann's shouts. A flash of grey – a pigeon? – shot from on top of Ann's chest into the rectangle of outdoor sunlight. The wall to the right, the entire wall of the flat, was gone.

'Tell me I'm dreaming,' Ann said.

He watched Ann throw off the covers and race to the gap, moving her hand in and out of the empty space, tracing where the corners of the walls should have met. The pensioners across the road were staring at her from their garden balcony. Instinctively, she gave them a wave. Then she glanced down at her underwear with horror. Putting his slippers and dressing gown on, Carl approached the void with less enthusiasm. He reckoned this was as good a time as any to skip his morning stretches. There wasn't a brick out of place to prove there'd even been a wall – no broken cement, no cracks, no nothing. He leaned out of the hole just far enough to see a slice of the inside of the room directly below theirs. Their wall was gone too. The whole side of the building was gone. While holding on to the edge of a remaining wall for support, he brushed hands with Peter from next door who was peering into Carl and Ann's bedroom. They both looked away too quickly. Carl struggled for the appropriate words demanded by small talk.

'That's a nice lamp you have there,' Peter said.

'Ah yes, I thought that last time I visited,' a voice called from above them.

Carl glanced up.

'Custard cream?' the voice asked.

Mrs Martinez, the neighbour directly above them, had propped herself on the edge of her floor, dangling her size 8 feet over and into Carl's ceiling space. Watching the old lady lean to drop biscuits into Ann's hands, he wondered if a fall from the sixth floor would kill her. Should he tell her to be more careful? Ann didn't seem to worry though. She was more interested in discussing Mrs Martinez's daughter's friend's pregnancy. Ann seemed gripped. There was no wall and here Carl was wondering if he could ask for another biscuit or maybe even sell the lamp to Peter. Things like this simply didn't happen. It wasn't right.

'Well I'm going back to sleep, even if you're not,' Carl called after Ann as she wandered into the kitchen, 'and get a dressing gown.' He wondered if this had happened because Ann had put the fan on before they went to sleep. Where was the fan?

Carl couldn't get back to sleep. He could feel the neighbours pointing at their flat, judging his pyjamas. He should have worn the new ones. He hoped no-one had seen the hole in his bed socks. The opinions of neighbours shouldn't have mattered so much. Pinching his arm didn't wake him up. If you pinch yourself in a dream do you pinch yourself in real life? Or did he need real Ann to wake him up? He should have studied psychology or something, not engineering.

'Bloody hell! Carl! The washing machine and counters have gone with the wall!'

At least it wasn't the fridge. When Ann came back in, she continued gossiping with Peter and Mrs Martínez's geriatric legs.

'Apparently, the caretakers are on it but,' Carl could hear Peter's snigger through the wall, 'of course, there isn't much they can do when a whole insulated wall's gone walkabout.'

'I suppose we're lucky it's summer,' Ann said, walking towards the night stand with orange juice for herself and water for Carl.

'So this still isn't a good enough time for coffee?' Carl propped himself up on his pillows, ignoring the stares coming from the building opposite.

'Think of your blood pressure.'

'That's salt.'

Ann began to tidy up. She picked apart her week old pile of clothes before asking the group, 'Hey, is a room with three walls still a room?'

'Don't try to be clever.'

Ann shushed him, deciding to continue her conversation with the two interlopers.

'Well you know what they say, as soon as you start wanting a child, you've given up on yourself...'

They still hadn't moved on from that girl's pregnancy, bestowing their infinite wisdom and experience on the matter. Carl had never realised Peter was such a gossip. He glanced at their own family photos. Ann always wanted to be dramatic, even if it meant being needlessly judgmental. She hadn't given up on herself after having the kids. She had her work. She was constantly dedicating herself to new hobbies and new opportunities. And yet, every day, she complained about the absence of calls from the girls. Beth was probably at work, even this early, and Amelia was wasting time at her boyfriend's place. That's what you get from an arts degree. He'd learnt not to say that sort of thing out loud.

'Don't you have work, dear?' the legs called down to Ann. Immediately Ann turned to Carl, her face frozen. The clock was gone with the wall, gone to tick somewhere else.

'It's 6.30,' Carl replied to her horrified facial expression, turning off the alarm on his phone. She still had time. But then there was the wall. Or lack of it. Did he call in sick at work? Saying 'Oh yeah, my wall's missing, seen it around?' Did they both miss work? He caught her eye and she said,

'This could be a nice excuse to pull a sickie.'

Of course she thought that. Carl eyed the clouds. If the rain came inside they would need to pull more than a sickie. He wondered how much protection a nailed duvet cover would provide.

'You realise we've got a lot to sort out?' Carl began, 'The electricity probably doesn't work and the water...'

She wasn't listening. She was eyeing the neighbours across the road. There was a young man she found particularly attractive in a flat opposite – she was always telling Carl that he reminded her of a younger version of him. Carl Jr. was out on his balcony, smoking. Or rather holding an unlit cigarette and a flaming lighter. He was evidently a bit slow on the uptake. He responded to Ann's wave with the energy of a sloth. Carl wondered if his own face was a bit calmer when noticing the lack of wall.

When Ann realised she was still in her underwear, she quickly leapt up from their new personal arena and opened the closet, pausing there for several minutes as she glanced between her clothing choices. By the time she had decided, he had finished sipping his water and called work. Ann went to get changed in the bathroom.

'I'm hardly going to change here where everything's on display,' Ann said.

When she came back, she automatically went to the space where the wall had been before remembering it wasn't there anymore.

'Where do you think the mirror's gone?' she asked.

It had to have disappeared somewhere. The mirror was probably where the curtains, the washing machine and everything else had gone – maybe in a big pile with neighbours' belongings. It would be like baggage claim in Jamaica all over again. Ann's luggage was never picked up by accident or lost in piles of monochrome, unlike Carl's. Her suitcase now rested safely on top of the wardrobe, one side a very streaky yellow. She had got bored by the time she'd painted half a side.

'It's probably with the wall,' Carl said.

'Yeah but where?'

'Well,' he tried to think logically, 'It could have fallen in the night and been removed before anyone saw. You know, health and safety...' Even he didn't genuinely believe this. He doubted if the eavesdropping neighbours would either.

Ann didn't appreciate his comment, dignifying it only with a very slow eyebrow raise and a, 'Well maybe this is a good thing.'

Typical.

'Are you serious?'

'Materialism isn't always a good thing,' Ann said.

'When is it...' Carl broke off and tried to continue more quietly, 'You know tomorrow they'll probably tell us it was some kind of construction flaw.'

'So the wall just fell off?'

All of a sudden he felt like one of the kids at her school.

'Oh come on, that's a lot more believable than the gods just vanishing it away so that we can learn some greater lesson. Don't be stupid.'

'Where's the wall then?'

Mrs Martínez stopped swinging her legs and attempted to lift them slowly back into her flat upstairs. Carl found himself hoping she wouldn't fall off. But also hoping for a distraction.

'What?'

He realised the old lady wasn't going to fall after all.

'If it just fell off, where is it then?' Ann leaned over the edge, mock-seriously investigating the street below. 'Why is it so hard for you to believe that there's some deeper meaning?'

'Because it's a wall.'

'You know what? I should have known you wouldn't understand.'

She slammed the bedroom door.

*

A week later, amid rumours of scaffolding and a new wall, Ann had started changing in the room, was waving to Carl Jr. and every passerby, was wearing thinner, tighter, more revealing clothes and pulling back the tarpaulin Carl had put up. She even bought newspapers to read.

'You know, if you want them to think you're clever, don't buy the *Daily Mail*,' Carl said.

She folded it away and went out to buy food. She even came back with coffee.

'You've finally learnt! I told you all along it was salt that was bad for me, not sugar,' Carl joked in triumph.

She put headphones on. Even though it was now the school holidays, she still marked the students' late homework, still deployed endless lines of gold stars. He never got any. She guarded them with frightening strength. But eventually she ran out.

'God's sake!'

'Maybe now you'll learn to ration them.'

'You know what?' Ann began. But she stopped herself. She put the papers to one side and turned the desk chair towards him and away from Mrs Martinez's permanent position with her legs drooping like dehydrated stems into their bedroom.

'Carl, listen. I think maybe it's time we talk.'

He chuckled, 'Am I in trouble?'

He wondered if there were any stickers for being mean.

'Why do you do that?' she said.

'Do what?'

'I'm not as stupid as you think I am!'

Carl glanced at the walls. They suddenly seemed permeable. Ann took a deep breath and tried to sit back. She watched Mrs Martínez's legs withdraw from their ceiling space.

'This whole set-up is just wrong. I keep telling myself that this is a phase but this phase has lasted, what, half the time we've been married?' She didn't even look at him. 'I just don't feel like I'm happy anymore. I've forgotten why I ever thought this was a good idea – was it the kids?'

'This'? What are you getting at?' Carl peeked at the self-help books on her side of the bed, searching for a manipulative title about middle-aged relationships. She caught him doing it.

'Stop it! Don't try to blame this on something else! Let me talk... ! Spending days together like this, with no work in between, no distractions –'

'What are you trying to say?' he raised his voice, daring her to do the same.

'It's just,' her eyes flitted across the room, checking that the neighbours in the building opposite weren't staring, listening for Peter's creaky floorboards next door before finally resting on Carl's eyes, 'The longer I'm with you the lonelier I feel.'

He should have said something, anything. But all he could feel were the eyes from the building opposite. The hole in his bed socks.

Magdalena Meza Mitcher

PASTEL COLOURED WINTER

The air tastes blue. Snowflakes float down and I imagine that the sky is shedding its thin summer skin for a winter coat. Droplets cling to my eyelashes, clutching them before falling onto my cheek. The grass is frozen, too. I grab a fistful of it and the ice crunches like teeth breaking, then melts away.

Water is bubbling, somewhere. I can hear it in the back of my mind; a memory of a place trying to grab my attention for a moment. I cock my head slightly, but I still can't place the stream. It's behind me somewhere, I think. It's quiet, patiently toddling along, taking the time to touch everything it comes to. I smile; I think the stream is like me. I like to imagine that it's trundling down the valley, picking up snowflakes on the way and taking them where they need to be. I feel like it might be sunny, and I pretend I can see the rays join the water on its journey. I picture the sunlight jumping in and out of the river like salmon in November, with glittering scales of crystal and gold.

I think a hand touches mine. A finger traces the veins on the back of my hand, as familiar as cinnamon and apple scented candles at Christmas. It's ice on skin, burning me from the inside out. The cinnamon and apple is coming from my own veins; it's a candle that's been lit in my heart and pulsates through my body.

You shouldn't be here. The voice comes to me, clear as a mother scolding her clumsy child for walking into an expensive shop and almost knocking something over. My head is still cocked but I can't find the voice. She's running fairy rings around me. I can see the mushrooms growing green and grotesque. They look like the gnomes back at the house, who have moss for beards and eroded smiles with eyes that don't stop staring but still can't see. The mushrooms expand in a cloud of grey and smoke, reaching for me with fingers that curl and twist with every breath I take.

I will not scream. They cannot touch me. They are just fragments of me. They are fragments of her. Their tendrils fall down in ringlets and try to convince me I'm home, but I know it's just ash. It's always just ash.

I lift my head and hang it above my heart like she tells me to. *Heart over hips, head over heart, and you are centred again.* I wait for the mushrooms to dissipate. I watch them start to shrink down, billowing like clean sheets when the bedding gets changed. Soon enough, they're melting into the snow and rising in steam.

When are you going to come in? The voice comes back. She finds her way through the haze and sits beside me. The hand is still touching mine. It's gentle and cold but it's soothing against mine. I try to find my voice to answer her, but my lungs are filled with dust, and trying to talk burns. I don't want pain right now. I want to sit and be with the river for a while longer.

Time passes by me. The snow has stopped, and I can feel the trees around me silencing themselves so they don't wake the river. My thoughts begin to trickle back to me, travelling first in brooks, and then in streams, rushing to get to the lake before it freezes over. A living room flickers into the light. *Should I save you some dinner?* The voice calls to me from the kitchen down the hall. I shake my head slowly; it's too late for dinner now. The voice doesn't answer. She doesn't protest. She just cries. That's what she does most days. Sometimes she shouts, other times she just sits and says nothing.

You shouldn't be here. The voice is firmer. I know where she is now. I finally open my eyes and have to blink to make sure they're open because I'm surrounded by darkness. The river runs around me on three sides, so I decide to walk towards the fourth. The grass is crisp and frosted; every step I take I listen to this brittle symphony until I see the house towering over the hill ahead. When I reach it, I notice every light but one is turned off. Today must be a crying day.

Key in the lock. Shoulder to the frame. Ice dislodges, and warmth greets you with cinnamon and apple kisses. Feet through, first the right, then the left. Kick off the mud and frost and whatever else lives on the underside of your boots. Deep breath, first word of the day. Trust that the smoke in your lungs has also gone to sleep and won't singe your voice. Keep telling yourself this.

'Hello?'

It's funny how silence snatches any sound it's given. One word, hollow and tinny, is called out and the darkness takes it in two hands, clutches it to its chest and keeps it there forever.

'Mum? You in?' She must be in the living room. I take off my coat. Unbuttoning it becomes the hardest task of the day; my fingers appear to have seized up. One button at a time. The cat saunters past me, as if telling me it's my turn to deal with her today.

Five minutes later I've given up with my coat. I walk into the living room, coat half undone, half buttoned up. She's sitting there, on the sofa. She looks like a renaissance painting. Her hair flows out of her in curls and quiet sadness. Her right arm rests on the side of the sofa, her beaten up phone sitting delicately in her hand, as if it has just been placed there to add depth to the picture. Her feet are propped up beneath her. Her left arm is bent behind her, fingers absentmindedly playing with at her curls, she pulls them, then releases them, before finding another curl to pull.

'You alright?' I sit in front of her, cross legged on the floor. Her eyes drop to me, staring but unseeing, just like the gnomes.

'Do you want me to make some dinner?' She won't eat it and neither will I but it's usually a good idea to ask. She blinks and notices me, then bursts out crying. Maybe it wasn't a good idea this time.

'I should be making you dinner. Have you eaten?' She knows I haven't. She wipes her nose and looks to the hall, as if willing her body to make its way there somehow.

'I'm not hungry.'

'Neither am I. I'm sorry. It's just been a bad day.' As if I hadn't worked that out. I smile, 'I know. I had a bad day too.'

She smiles back. Tears continue to creep down her face. They make me think of the snowflakes. 'Where did you go today?'

I pause. I don't remember where I went. I don't know how to tell her this.

'A field, about twenty minutes away. There was a river.' A memory drips into the lake, 'I was following it.'

She stops watching me to look at the phone in her hand. She stares at it for a few moments, as if it could tell her where I'd gone. She looks back at me, clearly not having found the answer she was looking for. 'Do you remember anything else?'

I shake my head. Maybe if I keep shaking it my memories will drop out. I smile at this idea.

'What happened today?' I look at the phone, pleading with it to stay quiet.

She glazes back over. I can tell from the darkness in her eyes that she can't see me anymore; she can only see the day she's just had. 'I don't know. He rang me a few hours ago. We were talking about going away next year, somewhere warm to get the cold out. We were laughing, and then I must have said the wrong thing because five minutes later I was crying and he was telling me I was a manipulative whore. Then it went silent.'

I think it's funny that she thinks going somewhere warm will get the cold out. We've got frostbitten bones.

'Nothing else? He's not called again or texted?'

Now she was shaking her head. Maybe she was trying to shake out the memories too.

'Do you want me to keep the phone tonight?'

She nods. She must be tired. I look at her and wonder when she last slept. The bags under her eyes are the same as ever. Her bottom lip is more chewed up and bloody than it was yesterday; he must have been worse than usual today. I sit up, tucking my feet under me and reaching for the phone. She watches me, eyes wide and bloodshot. She looks like my cat when I try to take a mouse away from her. I close my hand around the phone. It's hot, the battery burning through the screen. I feel my fingers start to thaw. I put it in my coat pocket. She keeps watching me.

'Why is your coat half open?'

I smile at the confusion on her face; confused is better than crying.

'My fingers were too cold from being outside all day, so they seized up and I couldn't undo my coat properly. It snowed.'

A smile finds its way onto her face, a shadow of a life before the cold killed us and left us for the river. She unfolds her legs from beneath her and lowers herself onto the floor with me. She undoes the rest of my buttons, her fingers pink and hot from having the heating on all day.

It's a simple moment.

I close my eyes and watch the lake before me. It breathes in and out, waves gushing out pictures of family dinners before him, days out to the zoo, a holiday somewhere warm. I dip my toe into the water, it's warmer than I thought it would be. He cannot reach us here. The lake is hidden; the trees line it thickly. No wind reaches here. The air is still and breathless, but it's not uncomfortable; it's the type of breathlessness that hits you when you look at someone and you know they love you, their body screams it at you, their eyes speak words the world can't think of. She is swimming in the lake, laughing. Her curls are wet and weighed down, but her eyes are free. She is smiling. She wants me to join her. I don't want to get wet because I don't have any spare dry clothes and it might get cold later, but the water is so warm I can't resist. I take the leap.

You jump and the water crashes down around you. You wait for it to hit but nothing comes. You are falling. The lake is gone and so is she. The trees lose their leaves, the sky is enveloped in unbreakable white. The air is blue, it twists around you, playing with you as you fall. You're the mouse now. You close your eyes; the world is easier to deal with when you can't see it. You try crying out, you try calling for help, but she can't hear you. She's somewhere else. Your voice doesn't come out louder than a whisper. You can see the ground. The earth is frozen and hard, and you can see him at the bottom, waiting. You cover your face with your hands, knees tucked up to your chest.

'What's going on? Where's your head at? Talk to me baby, I'm here.'

The voice reaches her hand out to you. Grasping for it, you feel fire on ice. Her hand meets yours.

'Mum?'

The phone rings. It's funny how the silence snatches any sound it's given.

Tamar Moshkovitz

RED LION / BLACK DOG

Every day is a stretching of fabric.

On the days you don't think
                you don't stretch.
                you don't have to.
Snug, you sit over a rollie
watching yourself dry out
        on the laundry line.
The wind takes you and you let it.

The thinking might shock you when
all of a sudden you feel yourself
                              stretch.
Over a pint of fine Norwich ale in the
Red Lion Pub under a
spitting April sky your mind wonders,
        rather it wonders in and you are reminded
                you are only wearing one layer.
                      it's all your name can afford.

They let dogs in this pub,
apparently.
Something tugs and you tug back,
lock your teeth onto its hind legs just as it scurries away
                                        and pull
until you feel baby teeth in your mouth and
the pigment has bled into your skin and
the ground is never steady enough for your
heart to have a regular
rhythm.

The thing tugging is a black dog with the moon on her belly
who never so much as snapped her teeth at you

                              when she was alive.
Tugging, laying with her head over one paw and her
    tail drumming a war-beat on the cool marble floor
           playfully, lazily.
           Handle her carefully or the fabric will tear.
           The rockets hadn't yet started falling but she
                    anticipates it, pulls you forward,
                         your heart
                    stutters not because of the
           rockets but because you are being dragged
              to near future and
                    away from your home and
                    away from the lazy war-beat and the
                              moon on her belly,
                    to days when the sun is too hot and shines
                       too long to allow it to glow, too long to let anger
                              cool down enough for the rockets to stop.

Over a pint of fine Norwich ale in the
Red Lion Pub under a
spitting April sky you sit and think about a dead dog,
your dead dog and you are no longer feeling
so snug,
fabric stretched out by the knowledge
that it is bulletproof but falls apart
                    at the first sign of rain.

Eilish Mullane

THE FELTON GREEN COUNTY WOMEN'S SOCIAL CLUB

KEY

– = An interruption at the end of a line/ Abrupt ending/unheard beginning to a sentence.
/ = Overlapping of speech.
<u>Words</u> = Exaggerated emphasis.

… = trailing off.

> *A crisp, clean 1950s living room in the American Deep South – around Georgia: the kind seen in Nuclear Testing Sites or on propaganda posters. Vases of flowers are placed throughout the house. A sleek, leather sofa sits centre-stage, no marks of wear and tear, as though brand new, although the design is a few years old at least (USA 1950s Dunbar sofa model 4907). An equally pristine armchair sits to the left of the sofa. A coffee table sits in front of the sofa, covered with perfectly iced cakes and regimentally cut sandwiches. A bright, white front door is stage left with a screen door in front of it. Upstage centre, there is a kitchen, as immaculately clean as the living space, with new, shining appliances, a SMEG fridge. A row of pristine counters obscure most of the kitchen from view. There is a set of white double doors leading to the kitchen, currently open. The door to the bathroom is stage right, but the bathroom is unseen. Staged family photos hang on the wall – there is one space missing where a photo has been removed, but it is not overly noticeable. A coat rack with a man's overcoat and hat, as well as a woman's purse by the front door. Staircase stage right, the top of which is not seen by the audience.*
>
> *LAUREL sits on the sofa, dressed in a smart floral dress and baking apron. She rests her head in her hands. EMMY stands with her arms folded, in an older, sturdier dress. VIVIENNE rests her hands on her hips, wearing a sleek, black dress. The dead body of a man, dressed in a suit and tie, lies centre stage; a sharp kitchen knife sticking out of his chest.*

VIVIENNE: Jesus, Laurel. When you said 'Come over early to help', I thought you meant with the frosting.

Laurel stands up abruptly and begins to pace. The women are silent for a moment.

EMMY: Tragic, to die like that...

VIVIENNE: I'll say.

EMMY: I wonder why he felt like he had to do it.

LAUREL: Emmy, you know I –

EMMY: End it in such a brutal way –

LAUREL: Emmy, I –

EMMY: No. No, you didn't. Don't you even try to say those words again.

VIVIENNE: So, what? We say he did it?

EMMY: He fought in the war. It got to him. Couldn't live with the pain.

VIVIENNE: People'll believe that?

EMMY: They did when James died.

Laurel and Vivienne stare at her.

VIVIENNE: It's the giant knife that'll raise questions. People fall on their swords, sure, but I don't think it's meant to be *that* literal. Besides, it'd be Hell to balance.

EMMY *(Sharply, trying to maintain calm)*: Well, what would you propose?

LAUREL: He left me.

EMMY: What?

LAUREL: He packed his bags. He skipped town.

VIVIENNE: People will believe that?

LAUREL: Perhaps less than they should, but it's more likely than anything else.

VIVIENNE: Okay, one deserter coming up. So, what now?

EMMY: Vivienne, go upstairs and pack a case. If Eddie left, he'd take things with him. Laurel and I will take care of the rest.

Vivienne exits up the stairs.

LAUREL: The rest?

EMMY: We can't just have him lying on the floor. Mary-Ann will be here soon, and so will Sylvie. We – You don't need them involved.

Emmy stands by the feet of the dead body.

(To Laurel) Grab his arms.

Laurel holds the arms, Emmy takes the feet. The two women carry the body into the kitchen, behind the counters. Emmy pulls the knife out of the man's chest, appearing from behind the counter.

EMMY: Have you got anything we can use to... keep him in?

Laurel pops up next to her.

LAUREL: Uh, I have some Tupperware containers?

EMMY: Anythin' bigger?

Laurel shakes her head. Emmy places the knife on the counter.

I suppose we can make do. You go get them, I'll figure out what to do with the head.

> *Laurel exits. Emmy finds a meat cleaver in the kitchen drawer behind her, and ducks behind the counter. Vivienne enters down the stairs, pulling a heavy suitcase behind her.*

VIVIENNE: Jesus, who knew Eddie was such a clothes horse?!

> *Vivienne drops the suitcase in the living room, and leans against the kitchen doorway.*

Want some help?

EMMY: *(Passive-aggressive)* Don't you worry yourself. Wouldn't want to ruin that nice dress of yours.

VIVIENNE: Alright. If you insist.

> *Vivienne walks over to the food on the coffee table and helps herself to a slice of cake. She reclines on the sofa and starts eating.*

If there's anything I can help with, you just let me know.

> *Enter Laurel, carrying a pile of precariously balanced Tupperware containers.*

EMMY: I think I have a plan. Pass those here. Come help me.

> *Laurel and the containers disappear behind the counter. Chopping sounds are heard. Vast amounts of blood splatter the white kitchen surfaces. Vivienne looks from the kitchen to her cake, and back again, before setting the cake down on the coffee table. She takes a cigarette from her purse and lights it. She smokes.*
>
> *Tupperware containers, filled with sections of flesh and blood are placed on the counter. Emmy and Laurel appear, covered in blood. They walk into the living area. Vivienne looks for a place to ditch her cigarette- she drops it into one of the vases.*

VIVIENNE: Oh Lord.

LAUREL: Is it bad?

VIVIENNE: Oh no, Honey, it's fine. I hear red is really in this season.

> *Vivienne pulls the case into the kitchen and shuts the door.*

LAUREL: *(To Emmy)* Come on, you can borrow one of Mother's old dresses.

VIVIENNE: Preferably something a little less Marti and a little more Monroe.

> *Emmy looks from Vivienne to Laurel quizzically. Laurel looks at the floor. Laurel and Emmy go to walk upstairs. There is a knock at the door. The three women look at each other.*

MARY-ANN *(Offstage)*: Hell-Hellooo? It's Mary-Ann. I brought pound cake, hope that's okay?

> *Laurel looks pleadingly at Vivienne, before walking upstairs, followed quickly by Emmy. Vivienne straightens her dress and opens the door, blocking the doorway with her arm. Mary-Ann, a young woman of around twenty-two years old, is on the other side, dressed in a knit cotton shirt and knife pleat skirt. She is carrying a slightly burnt pound cake. On seeing Vivienne, she seems shocked, but recovers quickly.*

MARY-ANN: Oh. Hi Vivienne. I. Uh. Is Laurel at home? She did say three, didn't she? I'm not inconveniencing anyone, am I?

VIVIENNE *(pause):* Well, now that you mention it you have caught us at a bit of a bad time. Poor planning on our part. You see, Emmy managed to spill *(short pause)* coffee over her nice dress, so the two of them are finding something else for her to throw on.

MARY-ANN: Oh, I'm awful, awful sorry. Should I come back later?

VIVIENNE: Coffee is <u>such</u> a struggle to handle. I'm not sure how long they'll be. Maybe it'd be for the best –

Mary-Ann looks sadly down at her cake and sighs to herself.

MARY-ANN: Okay. Well I – I guess some other time then.

VIVIENNE: I guess so.

Mary-Ann mutters something unintelligible, but she looks visibly sad. What was that?

MARY-ANN: I said there's always spilled coffee... or frostin' to be made... or... Whenever I – Uh. Whenever I try t – to spend time with anyone...

Mary-Ann trails off and begins crying quietly, trying to cover it up. Vivienne looks from Mary-Ann to the staircase, then back again. She sighs to herself and moves her arm away from the door.

VIVIENNE: On second thought, they really shouldn't be too much longer, it can't be <u>too</u> hard to find a new dress, after all. *(Pause)* Why don't you come on in and wait for them.

MARY-ANN: Really? You sure?

VIVIENNE: No... but – Come on.

Mary-Ann enters. Vivienne shuts the door behind her.

(Gesturing to the cake) Let me take that off your hands.

Mary-Ann hands the cake over to Vivienne and turns away to look around the room. Vivienne looks at the cake questioningly, before clearing a space for it on the coffee table.

Vivienne sits down on the sofa. Mary-Ann hovers awkwardly.

VIVIENNE: So, is that a family recipe or –

Vivienne pats the cushion next to her, indicating for Mary-Ann to join. She does so, but does not relax into the sofa as Vivienne does, instead sitting up straight, as though in school.

MARY-ANN: Uh. Yes. It's uh. My Great Aunt came up with it when she uh – she first got married. Whenever one of the girls in our family gets hitched, they – they get a copy of the recipe. It's like a tradition, y'know?

VIVIENNE: Sweet. Well, I'm sure it'll be just heavenly.

The two women sit in awkward silence for a moment, both staring at the furnishings around the house, instead of each other.

VIVIENNE: I'll just go and see how they're getting on. You help yourself to some cake or somethin'.

Exit Vivienne, up the stairs. Mary-Ann looks around the room. She picks up her burnt cake, comparing it to the others on the coffee table. She sets the cake back down and stands up. She wanders around the room, looking at Laurel's family photos and decorations. She makes her way over to the kitchen door. As she is about to open it, the other women appear, making their way downstairs. Emmy is wearing a garish, ill-fitting dress from the 1940's. She does not look amused.

LAUREL: I'm so sorry that took so long. Coffee is just nightmare fuel. *(Noticing Mary-Ann at the door)* Oh Honey, don't go in there! It's a real state and I'd like to keep up the illusion that I don't make a mess in the kitchen.
 Laurel steers Mary-Ann away from the kitchen and Mary-Ann, Laurel and Emmy sit on the sofa. Vivienne sits in the armchair.
LAUREL: Oh, and you brought cake! How lovely... ! What is it?
MARY-ANN: It's uh – it's a Pound Cake...
LAUREL: Ooooh. I might have to take summa that off your hands!
MARY-ANN: My aunt always says that the real secret is choppin' up the nuts real small and mixin' 'em in. She says it's a way to trick my cousins into eatin' somethin' sorta healthy, y'know?
 Laurel exchanges a look with the other women.
LAUREL: Oh, well, that's very sweet –
EMMY: Mary-Ann, Laurel's allergic to nuts.
MARY-ANN: Oh lord! I'm so sorry! I'm such an –
LAUREL: That's okay. You weren't to know, I appreciate the thought all the same. Most people only know 'cause of this God-awful, if you pardon my French, reaction I had a few years back before even I knew about it. Can't even touch the things now, seems to bring me out in all kinds of –
MARY-ANN: I'm sorry, I coulda poisoned you. *(Pause)* Also I'm sorry if I'm early I'd hate to think of you all rushing around on my account and I – I'm just sorry.
LAUREL *(resting her hands on Mary-Ann's shoulders)*: Not at all, if you hadn't shown up who knows what kind of a state we'd be in. *(Pause)* I say, if you have plans, stick to 'em. Start goin' back on your word and who knows what'll happen?!
EMMY: I agree. Precision is key.

Matthew Nixon

THE WALL IN THE WAVES

ONE

Lloyd had always told me the wall was a secret entrance to a hidden base. It was forbidden, like a fortress. And I'd always believed him. When we would play by the ocean, pretending to be explorers or pirates, I would look out over the waves at it and imagine what was kept inside. It must have been important. Why else would it be so far out at sea, protected by the tides which ceaselessly crashed together around it?

I'm not so sure it really is a base anymore. One day, after Lloyd asked me if I thought anyone had ever gotten inside, I asked my sister about it.

'For heaven's sake, George,' she said. 'It's just a wall. There's obviously nothing more to it, and I'm positive there's no way anybody could swim out that far anyway.'

Naomi spoke in a way that made me feel like an idiot. I tried telling her about the time Lloyd and me saw a boat sail out there, but Naomi told me it was probably just the council.

'It's been there as long as anyone in this town remembers, and it's almost certainly falling apart.' Naomi talked like she was giving a presentation, and planted her hands on her hips. 'I reckon they're thinking about how to safely tear it down.'

I felt my cheeks flush and decided I didn't want to tell Naomi anything more about the wall.

TWO

The next day I cycled over to Lloyd's house as soon as I finished my morning chores, and he tried to teach me how to take a penalty. I could never kick very well, but something excited me about playing with Lloyd. How did he keep so balanced as he swung his leg? How could he kick with so much power and such little effort?

Lloyd's uncle, who was a fisherman, was visiting for lunch. I'd met him, Mr. Makepeace, once before. He had told me about a great storm he fought through out at sea in the middle of the night. He lost all sense of direction, but when he returned, he had caught so much cod he didn't need to take his boat out for the rest of the week.

'Mr Makepeace?' I asked, once he finished his lunch.

'Listen lad, I'm no stranger. Call me David.'

'David Makepeace,' I said, and kept talking through his laughter. 'Have you ever sailed out to the wall off of Greatstone Beach?'

'Can't say that I have, George. Never really get much luck in those waters, they're way too close to the shore.' Lloyd's uncle had a rough voice – I think he was a smoker – but I liked it.

Before I could ask Mr. Makepeace anything else, Lloyd's mum started talking to him about something grown up, so me and Lloyd decided to have another kick about.

'Do you think your uncle would ever take us out on his boat?' I asked my friend as he set the ball down on the penalty spot.

'Fat chance.' He took his kick. I dived left, and the ball shot past me on the right.

'And he sends it straight to the back of the net!' Lloyd cheered, pretending to shout into a microphone as he ran around the garden. I noticed how his shirt jumped up and down with his body. As I picked myself back up I caught a glance at his pale hips as the shirt revealed his torso.

When the two of us stopped laughing, I tried to bring the topic back up.

'If he did take us out, we could see if there was an entrance to the wall?'

'Maybe. If we're lucky and he has a morning free. I doubt it. But I'll ask.' Lloyd spoke like he was practically a grown up.

'Really? You will?'

'Sure.' Lloyd said. 'But only if you can actually save this next penalty!'

THREE

That night I had a dream about the wall. I was with Lloyd. We were stood atop it, and I could hear the ocean swell around us. I could taste salt in the air at the back of my throat. No matter how hard I looked I couldn't see the shore. We were all alone.

Beneath my feet, the wall felt cold. It was covered in seaweed and moss, and the concrete was starting to chip away. There was just enough space on the top of it for Lloyd and me to run around, but when I peered over the edge, I couldn't tell if the wall was floating or secured to the seafloor. The waves were rich and animated.

'George, over here!' Lloyd yelled. His hair was blonder than usual, and when he said my name it sounded like he was singing.

I walked over to him and cautiously took a seat on the edge.

'Do you see it?' he asked, raising his finger to the horizon.

'See what?'

'There's a dolphin!'

And so there was. I sat with Lloyd and watched the dolphin in silence. I could feel the wind in my hair. It wasn't too long until another dolphin surfaced, and the two played together beneath a sun which looked as if it would never set.

Lloyd ran his hand through my hair, and then I woke up.

FOUR

I could smell bacon. Mum was humming along with the radio in the next room. I heard her call that breakfast was ready but I didn't move. Maybe if I tried hard enough I could go back to sleep. Back to the wall. To Lloyd. I let my head fall into the pillow but it didn't work.

'Children! Will you come and get your breakfast?' Mum exaggerated her knocks against the wall. 'Your eggs will go cold!'

As I dragged my feet across the cold tiles of the kitchen floor, all I could think about was the wall. The more I thought about my dream, the more I remembered seeing a hatch. But what was inside?

'Mum,' I said, between mouthfuls of toast. 'You know the wall out by Greatstone Beach, right?'

Mum knew everything, but before she could respond my sister sputtered out, 'Here we go again.'

'Yes dear,' Mum began, not letting Naomi speak. 'What about it?'

I felt the words run out of my mouth. 'Well Lloyd says it's a hidden base and I think it might be used by the army – either that or it's the Queen's, but Naomi doesn't believe me. What do you think? Oh! You know Lloyd's uncle is a fisherman? Well he kind of sort of said he will take us out there. Would that be okay?'

Mum told me to slow down, but I couldn't help it.

'I think it's called a Mulberry Harbour,' she explained. 'They built them ahead of a big battle in the Second World War. It's a sort of floating pier that they would take across the channel so the soldiers could bring their equipment to France.'

Mum must have noticed my fallen expression.

'But, I suppose if you were wearing a lifejacket, and he really wanted to, then I'd let Mr. Makepeace take you to see for yourself,' She looked me right in the eyes. 'Of course, that's only if your bedroom was tidy.'

I quickly left to make my bed and pack away my books, my heart beating fast the whole time.

FIVE

Going out to the wall with Lloyd was the only thought I entertained for the next two weeks. It was nearly all we spoke about at school, while playing football, or whenever we went past the beach. But when Lloyd told me one morning that his uncle finally said yes, I was nervous.

It occurred to me that I'd never been on a boat before. Lloyd was excited. He told me he wanted to lay this mystery to rest, but I didn't have anything to say. What if I was too scared to get on the boat? What if Mum was right? What if it was just a wall, and nothing more? Maybe Lloyd and me would lose out on something special.

That Saturday morning, there was a chill in the air. The cold wind brushing my skin and the twist in my stomach was all that kept me awake.

'Can you believe it?' Lloyd asked as we set out on his uncle's boat. 'We're actually going out to the wall. Aren't you happy?'

I said nothing, and looked out to the waves. They caught the sun's early morning rays and glimmered like stars.

'Full steam ahead. Watch out for pirates now, Captain George! Turn to the starboard side.' Lloyd's silly impression cheered me up for our rest of the journey. His jawline was sharp and his footing was steady as he peered along the horizon, searching for pirate ships with a telescope made out of his hands.

'Not far now, lads,' I heard Mr. Makepeace shout from behind his wheel. 'There she is.'

And there 'she' was. And she was just a wall, but I didn't care anymore. I realised that, for the last fifteen minutes, all I had done was watch Lloyd. Wearing his uncle's hat, pretending to be a captain, there was something captivating and warm about him. Something that made me feel safe, and easy. Suddenly, it was like I was dreaming again.

We circled the wall once or twice in silence, taking in all its crusty details.

'Well, George.' Lloyd's voice was music. 'We might have been wrong about this one. There's no secret entrance.'

'Either that,' I said, not sure what to believe. 'Or it's so well hidden we can't find it.'

Alyssa Ollivier-Tabukashvili

AT FIRST SIGHT

It was Thursday, 8th January, when we started the treatment. A beautiful rose on my thigh, so intricately done over five hours, only to be torn apart again over six weeks. He said it would take several weeks to get rid of because of the coloured layers.

'Anna, may I ask, why do you want this removed? It's a nice tattoo.'

I stumbled on that one.

That first session had come after a consultation a month before. I had noted in my journal how his teeth were so perfectly aligned when he smiled. I didn't mention that you couldn't see his chipped tooth in the pictures.

I mean – the picture in the reception.

I was looking forward to the treatment sessions. I expected they would be twice as painful as the initial ink, but once I met the practitioner I figured I'd handle them fine. When he passed the paperwork to me in the consultation his hand grazed mine and I felt a spark run through my veins like in a film.

We couldn't really converse during the treatments but I felt I knew all there was to know about him anyway. While the beam ripped apart the ink in my thigh I watched Fabio's relaxed visage: a quintessential Mediterranean face, its dark brow veiling a southern warmth. The eyes maintained the same pierced focus through the goggles as in the pictures.

The pictures in the reception's brochure.

I suppose it might have seemed strange to take so many of those leaflets with his face. In three sessions I got nineteen of them. I would tell the receptionist, 'I'm referring this place to a friend,' pinching a couple each time in and out, sliding them into my 'FF'.

That's 'F' for folder.

There was this one day between the third and fourth session when I found – bumped into – Fabio in his local independent café, *Café Louistic*, owned by a Franco-Algerian couple. He ordered a mazagran coffee with extra lemon and sat at a table near the notice board. I didn't order but leaned over to pin a random leaflet from my junk mail, knocking his table. He half-raised his head from the newspaper, 'Ah, Anna it's you. You're in this area?'

'No my si... cousin lives around here.'

I hurried out of the café, I didn't expect to be so nervous the first time he was seeing me outside of the clinic. I scribbled notes about everything that went wrong. Pinning that random leaflet as if I cared about whatever company it was. Almost saying 'sister' when Fabio knew from the previous session I was an only child. Getting nervous. Pretending I had a cousin living there. Running out.

As I placed the notes into the folder a tall, curly-haired woman walked by and turned into *Café Louistic*. She had a long stride with an easy gait: despite the January frost she was lightly layered, as if spring followed her everywhere. Her grace made a lump grow in my throat and unease swelled in my chest.

I followed the steps she'd taken from the street corner to the café. His sister? He did mention one and she had the same dark, curly southern European hair. Or his wife? No. I put that out of my mind immediately: he had no wedding ring and I would have seen them together before. I told myself to stop being crazy and consider that she could have no connection to him whatsoever. She was probably just going to sit down at a separate table, drink some coffee and read. That thought didn't stop me from walking to the café window. My entire body sank. I felt my ribs and stomach scrunch together as I watched Fabio put his arms around her in a warm embrace. I stepped back and went home.

I decided to ignore the *café incident*, as referred to in my notes. Well, first I crumpled onto my carpet, drank too much wine, and tore apart the 'Fabio Wall' I had worked on all that time. Almost *three months* of creating it, with polaroid snaps of him in the places I'd seen him, the brands he liked, his grocery habits and cut-outs of his face from the clinic's leaflets onto magazine pages and film stills – it was nice to imagine him out of his white coat, holding my hand on a walk along the beach. Half of these resources were from November, before the consultation – his first time meeting me – had even taken place.

It was crazy how easily it could come apart after so much effort.

Sitting among the leaflets, notes and polaroids, I finished my wine and thought about that day. I thought about disappointment and how this wasn't the first instance. Curled up in my shirt and knickers, my empty stare fell on the fading tattoo. The thorns were still darker than the rose petals.

And then I thought about how irrational I was. The woman could have been a friend. Or even a date but that didn't mean he was in love with her. Maybe she had a crazy quirk that would turn him away.

I told myself I could bet on that hope, or that I could charm him more. I started putting my Fabio wall back together, adding my new relic from that day: his receipt from the counter. The reasonable thing to do would be to outright ask him in the next session if he was seeing anyone. There were only three sessions left.

But I didn't ask. The entire hour I bit my lip, from the discomfort of the laser but also from the rush of his palm at the top of my thigh. When finished, Fabio went to get more antibiotic cream from the stockroom. His calendar was open to that week on the desk. I sat up on the bed, my legs bare and the rose half as pigmented as it was four weeks ago. I don't know why I chose that rose, why get a nice tattoo knowing you'll have it removed?

I didn't go home at the end of the session.

Opposite the clinic was a book shop with a coffee bar. I sat with my book in a green armchair by the window, crouching whenever someone walked out of the clinic.

I waited for Fabio to finish his working day. His calendar said his last appointment was at four o'clock. Five-fifteen came and he was outside. I followed him to the end of the street and turned left a few steps after him. I changed my jacket and let my hair down just in case. I felt myself sweating more at every turn until we finally reached a row of houses. I froze on the end of the street; seven houses down, he turned.

The next day I followed him again, waiting thirty minutes for it to get dark. I walked seven houses down. It was a relatively quiet street, some cars driving by every now and then.

I waited outside Fabio's house around a dozen times during those last two and a half weeks of sessions. There was no life in the front rooms in the evenings, no one else seemed to come in or out during the day. In the penultimate session, I memorised his schedule for the following weeks from the planner on his desk.

On Friday the 6th I was outside again. He had consultations and removal sessions until 6; I pushed away the image of him gently pressing the skin on other women's thighs and backs. I was almost paralysed by the sight of his house before me in daylight, empty and unguarded. I hesitantly placed one foot onto the front path, as though it might crumble like a trap floor. It didn't. I peered into the window of something like a living room; it was hard to tell what lay behind the mesh curtain, my view was blocked by the backs of frames on the ledge.

I found a small window on the side of the house. I leapt up and held onto the window pane with all my strength, raising myself enough to get a look inside. It was the bathroom. Though tidy, it was a weird place for photos. There were more frames on the cabinet, the wall, a couple on a bathroom organiser too. I pictured myself in those frames, caught in my own habits, maybe in shops or even at home. Maybe one day they'd be pictures together on a sunny beach like the ones I had cropped his face into.

I dropped from the window, satisfied for the day.

And then it was February the 14th.

I had scavenged the front garden for a key: under the door mat, in the flower pot, in the *fake* flower pot even, and in the garden light. But there was nothing. I slid around the side of the house and searched the bushes: there was a small meter box. From my bag I dug out two hairpins and began the job of scraping the lock's pins until its little door gave way. Army dads teach you the strangest things.

From the cabinet's corner, I took what looked like a house key.

The key slid into a newly-oiled lock and turned twice before the door opened, welcoming me. I took several steps until I was completely immersed. I felt a chill in my ribs, sides and spine: this was a new level.

My heart stopped as I realised – maybe this was disappointment again. Maybe he was another creep or had 'commitment issues'.

But then, I remembered how it felt to have Fabio near me, his hands touching, examining the progress before the laser apparatus could prick at my skin.

It was going to be a cheesily romantic surprise, but no other day in the year could forgive you for it.

In our last session, I thanked him for the treatment. I had worn a low-cut shirt that day. His jaw clenched at the name inked on my sternum.

'How man – ahem... do you know?'

I smiled at that.

Inside was clean and orderly like the clinic: plain without frills or embellishments. A single man's home. I was surprised there weren't more picture frames.

I tiptoed upstairs, letting a handful of rose petals fall decoratively. There were only two doors upstairs: I was led to the furthest one. I opened it and found the master, Fabio's, bedroom. I sprinkled the petals everywhere until I saw the picture frames on the night table. Coming closer I recognised the woman from *Café Louistic* and, beside her, a young girl with the perfect Mediterranean blend of Fabio and the woman.

Then there were voices outside.

I tossed the 'secret valentine' card onto the bed and hurried to the landing. The voices weren't muffled.

'I don't know who, officer, but my meter box is open and the key is gone.'

I ran for the other upstairs room and checked the window. Outside was Fabio. And two policemen. I turned, looking for a hiding place.

And then I saw the photos.

That same woman. Her elegance stabbed me from every angle in the room, shrinking me into anguish. I pulled my V-neck down to look at my new ink; the mirror showed red skin, a cursive 'F' etched between my breasts.

Three months ago, a leaflet. So only in films did love come at first sight.

'ANNA?' Fabio was calling me. 'Is it you?' He *wanted* me.

'Annalise, we can work this –'

No.

In the frame, Annalise mocked me. I listened to Fabio's footsteps coming up the stairs. He stopped. I waited. Waited for him to open the door, hopeful for Annalise but only finding Anna.

The silence on the stairs tasted like the cranberries my father stole. Among the silence was my heart, screeching against its skeletal cage, and his gentle breaths on the staircase.

Henry Opina

SO FAR SO GOOD

The evening I was born
and cut from my umbilical cord
they spanked me and I cried.   so far so good.

They gave me a name and it was all I could say
because my day dreams weren't in English yet
I tried to speak in colour
but they mistook my blue but
with every cry came food so   so far so good.

And when I ~~caught~~ could speak
I thought politeness was a magic word.
I pray you to please me. Please, please,
'Please. I should be allowed to play with fireworks
if they're the colour of my sherbet straws
and made the sound of your belt
when I push too far with my demands.'

But that's how love is taught
even if I'm too young to understand
yet   so far so good.

The sky at night isn't actually black
just a darker blue than the sky at day
and with that knowledge in mind
there's nowhere I can go that isn't   so far so good

'til I ventured far enough to where I couldn't see the sky
for I mistook her silence for another shade of blue
and I mistook her tears to be a cry to give her food
Because what I mistook for loving her,
what I mistook as just

was just
so far so good.

Henry Opina

BLEED

Have you ever followed where a moment bleeds?
                       where your hair runs like melted chocolate on the sky
                   beside you. Where the clouds could drip like ice cream
and
                           stain the sleeve of your red hoodie, or rather
my red hoodie on your shoulders.

That is where the moment bleeds to: The sleeves of the hoodie I now wear in winter still
                   stretched out from when it was tied around your waist.

                             Retrospect is finding clarity in
the distant heat haze. Clutching the black plastic strip of film that we dipped
                    in the summer
                 in a second
           we caught the sun as
       it was dripping down the back of your hand
     the moment bled and
   the hoodie was sky coloured
   and the Cromer sky was red.

As I'm watching the sleet with
my sleeve on my mouth to
filter out the hot dust we puff
into our crowded buses so that
we don't feel the chill of winter,
I'm drawing seagulls on the fog
on the windows as I'm passing by the station
where we waited for that Cromer train on the wrong platform.
     And even when it is the right platform,
         I still feel we're meant to be
                 two platforms down.

Cara Ow

NAME

when I was born	I was given two names
body built to bend	between split states

the English self doesn't come with instruction
it appears quite simply and means the same thing
across your American 'A' and your British 'Ah'
Cara (or Cara)
always remains.

the Chinese self mandates its meaning
shū is sung with gentle force a woman, a lady
pushing flat and thin from behind my teeth
yí rises slow like a smile drawn from my belly
it's only in the strict softness of these tones that I do exist

I haven't had much practice in a long while
body off balance I spit my Mandarin self out
harsh little daggers thrown from my mouth
I kill my self over and over in deafness of tone
each time dying unforgiven on newer English lips

Georgina Pearsall

SHOWERS

She stood on her doorstep wrapped up in the pre-dispositional lines of illness. They coiled back through her family history, in long sabbaticals to special facilities, in rehab centres and NHS counsellors. If you had asked how she came to have her second mental breakdown, she would have said she tripped into it.

Like a mother traumatised by a C-Section, she was determined to have the second one at home. 'Home' was her grotty rental place. Her stop-gap, five years out of university and three years into her stop-gap job, in her temporary neighbourhood with her temporary friends, with her roommates who she had at one time sincerely liked.

She removed her shoes at the door. No one was home. It was a Wednesday afternoon, three hours before the end of the workday. She dropped her coat in the doorway, unbuttoned her shirt and dropped it on the stairs. Her bra tumbled down after it as she unzipped her skirt and let it fall in the bathroom doorway, she discarded her tights and her underwear in the sink with her handbag. Soap scum and stale water soaked into the suede and the polyester.

She turned on the shower and stepped into the cold, flexing her toes. She loaded peach-scented shower gel into a loofah and washed mechanically as the water warmed. She repeated the action three more times, then kicked the loofah to the end of the bathtub where it nudged the stained edge of the shower curtain. The curtain was decorated with inspirational quotes: true beauty comes from within, you are in a beauty contest every day of your life, if you got it flaunt it. What was it? 'It' might well be no prospects and crushing mental illness, and how to flaunt that was not overwhelmingly clear. She fiddled with the temperature dial and picked out the least rusty razor. Because everyday life felt like a beauty contest and she was not certain her internal beauty was bright enough to shine through without a little help, she shaved her legs.

A year ago, after an argument with her landlord via email and then when he had stopped replying, through heated telephone calls, she had advocated for and received a new compact combi boiler. It was the type that heated the water as it went, rather than filling a tank of precious and increasingly scarce copper with cold water and letting it fill with metal ions and rust before heating it all, when only half of would be used by the end of the day. The environmental benefit was astronomical. It also meant she could take a bath without disrupting the erratic 3am showers of her housemates.

She had to wash her hair. She shampooed twice for the first time in ten years. Then she would have to let the conditioner soak in well. To replace the oils she would wash out with the second lot of shampoo. It was the cheap, nasty stuff, too, the kind she bought when the walls were closing in and she had to get out of the supermarket as quickly as possible. This process would take half an hour, at least.

As a child, she had loved showers. That was before showering was work. As an adult she had to shave and scrub and condition, as well as using two face washes to get the dribbling mascara off of her cheeks. Her father still joked that he hadn't had a hot shower since she had been born, because when left to her own devices she would stay in the shower until the tank emptied and the water faded from lukewarm to cold. Moderation was not her strong suit.

She would have to move home. Not today, though. She found the comb she kept in the shower, a cheap hunk of plastic with half of the teeth snapped off. She reapplied the conditioner with the help of the comb. This took time and cost her a few chunks of hair that she didn't need. Another thirty minutes to really get it smooth.

In the sink her phone rang. She peeked out at the vibrating handbag, hiding behind the curtain, hands clasped around the neon text proclaiming that her imperfections were beautiful. She dropped the curtain, pulling it tight to the wall as a protective barrier, dug out the exfoliating glove she had received in a gift set circa 2009, and proceeded to scrub half of the skin off of her torso. Christmas 2009. The famous row. Her dad was drunk out of his mind by midday and explaining to her at length why she was an idiot for not going into science, and that she might have had a shot as a writer in another universe, perhaps one where she had stumbled upon some talent too.

She heard the usual six o'clock rallying cries of her returning roommates through the hiss of the water. She would have to talk to them, ask how their days went, endure the questions about why her clothes ran the length of the house. Why was she home? They knew that she worked until seven most days, and that Wednesday was date night. It wasn't night though, it couldn't be; she was still in the shower. Behind an incredibly tacky curtain she had created a space outside of time. A much safer place to be.

Her phone continued to ring. It was joined by someone knocking at the door. A muffled voice. She called out:

'I can't hear you – I'm in the shower.'

Her saturated fingers had lost most of their sensation, but this would only be a problem when she got out of the shower. So far, she had no plans to do so. If she stuck it out for another six hours or so, her phone would run out of battery. Particularly if it kept vibrating like that. Maybe in four hours she would be able to enjoy the sound of nothing but the power-shower humming. She hummed along trying to match its pitch. Was it a C? Maybe a C flat. She ought to have stuck with the singing lessons. The acoustics were good enough that she might finally have time to practice. So she did. As a part of her choir she had an hour-long concert prepared, which she happily went through without the pressure of having to ever perform it for a crowd.

More knocking interrupted her at the very moment she finished. Her hair had started to clog the drain, but no one else ever cleaned it, and it was not her turn to unblock the thing. She poked at it with her toe.

'You've been in there for two hours now,' a voice called through the door. Five hours, actually. 'We were wondering when you might get out? Lily rang. She's worried about you. Said your mum called her. I could ask her to come over?' Lily or her mother? Both options were horrifying.

'Do I bother you while you're in the shower?' She shouted, 'I haven't even washed the conditioner out yet!' This was true. It had started to congeal in her hair, like putty.

'Is everything okay?' the voice called. She was silent. 'Is that your phone?'

'Wouldn't know, I'm in the shower.'

'You can't stay in there forever.' Of course she could; she had the power of the new boiler behind her. 'I'm going to turn the boiler off, okay? You have half an hour.' So, he was a traitor then.

Through the thin walls she heard his footsteps retreat. She went over the middle section of the concert whilst applying a face mask. The showerhead sputtered, and the water turned ice cold. She put the plug in to soak her feet. The low water pressure meant it would take at least forty-five minutes for the water to come up to her shins, but she had all the time in the world.

'Come on, this is ridiculous,' came another disembodied voice, 'your boss called, Lily won't stop calling, your mother found our home number – I didn't even know we had a home number – look, I get what's happening.' He paused. 'Just think of the water bill at least.'

As if they knew how to pay the water bill. She was the one who set the account up.

Stopping her personal concert, she caught the end of their conversation.

'– you have the landlord's number, right? He has to know where the water shut-off valve thing is.'

She caught her head under the shower spray in her shock, flinching at the cold as the water carried away half the face mask and a dollop of conditioner. It hung on top of the water now gathered to her calves, a greasy film, bubbling slightly under the insistent flow of the water.

Someone rattled the door handle. The lock was cheap; it wouldn't hold out for long. They had proven before that it could be undone with a coin. In a last rebellion as the showerhead sputtered to a stop, she sunk into the water, her added mass causing it to spill over the side and soak the floor.

That was where they found her. Her ex-girlfriend's face laced with a mix of pity and sympathy, her housemate's detached eyes and her mother's half-scared half-contemptuous stare. She was huddled defiantly underwater, bleeding out coloured soap.

Johnny Raspin

THE BAD BATCH.

You were taken from under your mother and now you eagerly wait. The great transporter's backside draws near. *Beep beep.* It is like music, the melody of your dreams. *Beep beep...* You know what it means, the great transporter is here to facilitate your life's purpose. Its metal shell reflects the radiance of the Great Yolk that hangs in the big blue.

The Great Gold Yolk that bursts and spills its runny rays seems to deeply affect the giant softies. You have noticed that they consistently groan when the Yolk is hidden behind the big blue's fluffy pillows. Indeed, the Yolk appears to be an essential aspect of life.

This never surprised you.

You will miss your home, but you are too excited to feel any real sadness. The great transporter stops just shy of the entrance and becomes silent. One of your yolklings seated next to you wiggles with joy.

'Can you believe it? I've been waiting for this day and now it's finally here. I'm so happy I could crack!'

All twenty-three of your yolklings are equally enthused. 'I wonder which giant softy's house we will end up in,' one squeals above the rest.

'I don't really care about that. I'm more interested in what our giant softy is going to use me for,' another remarks.

'I hope I make them happy,' a third sighs reverently.

'You're all idiots,' an angry voice travels forward from the back of the batch, 'I don't understand what the hell you are all so happy about?'

'Here they go. Oh woe is me.'

'What? I'm just pointing out the truth.'

'And what's that then?' You begin to snigger with the rest of the batch.

'You laugh, but you're all blind. Blind and stupid. You're all going to be eaten and crapped out! That will be your legacy.'

'That's not true, we will be remembered for our service!'

'Remembered?! I can't believe that I'm stuck here with a bunch of half-formers. I was destined for great things you know, I was going to be just like my dad, not some giant softy's food.'

'Ha, they're deluded, they think they're a fully-formed. You're not kidding anyone, mate. You had no dad. If you did, you wouldn't be here.'

'I am a fully-formed. Or, at least, I was meant to be.'

'Well you're the most half-former looking fully-formed I've ever seen,' one of your yolklings sneers.

'Yeah? Well you're a useless crackpot! I hope you give your big softy the squits!'

Astonishment overruns the batch. Some begin to wail, 'why would they say such an awful thing,' while a number of others attempt to leave their seats. 'Let me smash him, let me smash him,' they cry.

Through the tumult, a voice of reason rises, 'If that's truly your opinion then do us all a favour and keep it to yourself. As for me – and I'm sure I can speak for the majority, I'm going to do exactly what I know is expected of me – *stay sunny side up.*'

Whatever, no good can come from talking to half-formers anyway.'

The back of the great transporter is opened by a giant softy, and you are transferred into its belly. Moments later, you are flung into darkness and the great transporter begins to shake and rumble, sending vibrations through the batch. It is cold within its bowels, but you know that there is no use complaining because the new home you will soon acquire is of a similar temperature. That is what Mother told you. Mother kept you warm. Mother cared for each of her children. You remember what she told you before you were taken.

'I'm sorry my child, I'm sorry that I couldn't give you more of a life. I tried, but I couldn't find you a father; all the cocks were limp that day... Oh what am I saying, just ignore me, I'm getting all sentimental again. Mothers can be selfish creatures. It's just that I would have loved to have watched you grow and become strong, but what I want isn't important. We all provide in different ways for the giant softies, and sometimes I forget that your purpose is just as important as those who stay here with me. Always remember that serving the giant softies is the greatest joy you will ever be granted. So, go forth my child and fulfil your purpose. Make your mother proud and always remember that I love you.'

You think to yourself that it would have been nice to have felt your mother one last time before leaving, for her to look at you with pride as you triumphantly go forward to fulfil your destiny. The great transporter begins to move.

'Here we go,' one of your yolklings gasps.

You are only moving for a short while before you come to a stop and the great transporter once again falls silent. The batch begins to whisper, 'Are we here? Oh my goodness, this is it.' All fall silent and listen intently to the giant softy leaving the front of the great transporter. They are emitting some kind of high-pitched noise. This merry tune resounds over and over, slowly fading away.

One of your yolklings behind you, somewhere in the middle of the batch, seems to be nattering away to themselves. You cannot be sure.

'Would you please shut up.

I didn't say anything.

Why lie? You know that I know that you did.

Look, there's no need to make a big deal out of it, all I thought was that I don't feel completely right about us being here.'

Why would you think something like that? For goodness sake you know how I get. We're already different enough, I don't want them thinking we're like that... deluded freak at the back...'

The voice from the back of the batch barks, 'I'm not bloody deluded you bastard!'

'Great, look what you've done, the attention is on us now.
I'm sorry that I said anything, I was just thinking out loud. It's really nothing to worry about, I'm sure our giant softy will love us. I've heard that they celebrate difference.'

One of your yolklings sighs, 'guys, I think we've got a doubler in the batch, they're going to think that we're all rotten at this rate.'

'No, no, you've, you've got it all wrong, we're just like you. I mean, damn it, I'm just like you.
I think you should stop talking now.
Don't tell me what to do.
Oh would you just shut up.'

'Right, that's it, let's get this doubler out of the batch. If you just... wiggle a little... that's it.' The batch begins to wriggle from side to side in an effort to dislodge the doubler.
'No please!
Come on guys, we're all friends here, there's really no need for this kind of behaviour,' the doubler pleads, when the back of the great transporter swings open...

The giant softy jumps in and heaves your batch up into their arms to carry you out carefully. The most extravagant coop you have ever seen appears, and standing at its entrance is another giant softy, your giant softy! They look pleased at your arrival. You are close now, you can almost taste victory.

But then disaster strikes. The giant softy carrying you trips and two of your yolklings fall from their seats; they hurtle towards the ground screaming. However, it is not until they hit the path and their shells are smashed, guts spilling, that you realise who they were.

The doubler's two golden yolks lie decimated, but what is even more disturbing is the realisation that the self-proclaimed fully-formed was indeed not lying. The batch's gasps are followed by a grave silence as a fledgling – bloody, featherless, dead – slides out of its cracked shell.

The two giant softies argue before you and the remainder of the batch are

carried back into the belly of the great transporter.
　'What's happening?' One of your yolklings sobs.
　'We were so close,' a forlorn mutter nearby drains the last of your hope.
　A bad batch. No purpose. Just a bad egg.

Ellie Reeves

ASTRAEA

When I was young my mother told me to watch my
mouth for black spots if I swore.
Mangoes taste rotten once they're licked by fruit flies.

She bought charcoal toothpaste when I failed to comply
to scrub out the black spots until my gums were raw.
When I was young my mother told me to watch my

mouth for apples with a taste for young teeth, deny
and try to stop milk whites littering the floor.
'Mangoes taste rotten once they're licked by fruit flies'

meant more as more teeth fell out, and dry
lies flaked off around my blooming lips when I swore.
When I was young my mother told me to watch my

mouth, it's open, it's inviting. You'll catch flies. Never trust a red
sky in the morning. The night stained it with white spores
because mangoes go rotten behind closed doors.

My mother has a daughter with her mother's taste for lies
but time and a still spotless mouth reassure.
When I was young my mother told me to watch my
mangoes. Mangoes are fruit. Fruit can go rotten and fruit
flies are fruit flies.

Ellie Reeves

FORTY DAYS AND FORTY NIGHTS

There's a house with a flesh roof
pulled taut and waterproof
but there's a gap in the kitchen floor
through which yellow mud starts to pour
pressing hands make the bedroom door groan,
soon the beating bed will be split bone.

There's a house with a flesh roof
rafters sweat as ingrown hairs fuse
worming away from melting glass
she pumps in pints of yellow gas
bubbling porcelain, pop. Her frothing flood
cleaves the bed and dries its blood.

There's a house with a flesh roof
a creature inside but we have no proof
Jenny looks away as the yellow house groans
when she bites down teeth hit brick and bone
Jenny's flood will drown the creature to ash
Jenny won't be waterproof as she takes out the trash.

Ellie Reeves

WRITTEN WITH A RENTED HAND

Maybe we should have guessed
maybe the silence should have tapped us on the shoulder and smiled just a
little as it stretched us out
maybe we should know the difference between a mirror and a window
but as the night rocks on the train they look so similar
the face in glass, potholed by tearing trees and orange stars,   looked like me
and yours looked like you   and we stared at them on our way
as our way of shrugging off the silence that tapped our shoulders.
Scratch that. We did guess but
you couldn't say because
        you left your mouth in Berlin and
                you couldn't breathe a word because
                        you left your lungs in Prague
and as for me
I left teeth in the Sagrada Família to
        bite down when it's complete to
                eat something other than my words. Sandstone tastes just as
bitter.
Our eyes watch us leave the train and take up four seats
take with them our ability to see where
                we're
            going.
~~Scratch that.~~ I guessed when
we played Frisbee with your heart in Hyde Park
I hid it to make you laugh   I could go get it.
I would go get it, but I leant you mine, with interest, and
knowing me I'd leave my feet under a table half way.
~~Scratch~~ that. I guessed but
suddenly
I couldn't give a
shit I dropped my bowels with an empty thud
down a staircase in Madrid
the rest we rung out despite its stubbornness
in a bedroom in Rome
left the red sheets for the cleaners it's time to go home to
                                      ~~scratch~~ that.

Fiona Sangster

INDEPENDENCE DATE

'1.01: PILOT'

TEASER

Fade in.

INT. LABORATORY – MIDNIGHT – 1977

Three men dressed in lab coats with the NASA symbol emblazoned on the back circle round a single, giant computer. One has grey hair, DR HARPER. Another is young, DR SAMSON. The third is middle aged with a beard, DR MARRON.

We don't see the computer, only their faces lit up by the screen as they stare at it.

DR SAMSON: Can't we make his dick a bit bigger?
DR HARPER: That's not what the mission is about, dear boy. This is the first real chance we have to continue the legacy of humanity. Long after we are all dead and gone, there is still the chance that beings from other planets will seek out the human race, and it's all thanks to us.
DR SAMSON: Yeah, but, look at it.
   He reaches out to touch the screen and Harper slaps his hand away.
DR SAMSON: I don't want aliens thinking about us like that. What if there's chicks? They're not going to want to come to our planet if they think we're lacking.
DR MARRON: I think he's quite handsome.
DR HARPER: Please, Dr. Marron, it's only the seventies. It's still weird that you're gay.
DR SAMSON: Almost okay, but not quite.
DR MARRON: Just saying. So, are we done? Can we burn the record?
DR HARPER: Yes. We're done.
DR SAMSON: Are you sure one Chuck Berry song is enough?

DR HARPER: Too many in my opinion.
DR MARRON: Okay, I'm sending it.

> *Marron presses the enter button on the computer. The room shakes. A golden record pops out of the front of the computer.*

DR HARPER: Why is it gold?
DR MARRON: I thought it would be cool.
DR HARPER: Okay, let's get to this base before dawn, I'll take it now.

> *He takes the record carefully and places it in a sleeve, which has the words 'VOYAGER RECORD (IF YOU HADN'T ALREADY GUESSED)' on it. Marron leaves the room.*
>
> *Harper and Samson stare at the screen.*

DR HARPER: He's not that cute, now that I look at him.
DR SAMSON: Ew.

> *We see the screen from behind the scientists – the image of a nude man and women from the Voyager Golden record.*
>
> *Fade out.*

END OF TEASER

ACT ONE

TITLE: INDEPENDENCE DATE

INT. RESTAURANT – EVENING – SATURDAY, 7PM

> *A mid-range Italian restaurant. The BUZZ of people. Dim, romantic lighting and candles on tables. Soft PIANO MUSIC in the background. We follow a SERVER as she walks through the restaurant, and approaches a small table. Two place settings are laid out but only one sits there – MARIA, a 33 year old woman with dark brown hair, dressed plainly but elegantly. She nurses a white wine, frowning.*

SERVER: Would you like a refill, ma'am?
MARIA: No thank you. Could I get a glass of water, please?
SERVER: Of course.

> *The server gives her a tiny sympathetic smile as she walks off. Maria checks her phone – 7.10pm. She sighs and pushes her wine away from her.*

CUT TO:

INT. RESTAURANT BATHROOM – CONTINUOUS

> *A man with sandy hair is bent over a sink, washing his face. As he stands we see his face in the mirror – this is JIM, 36, handsome but haggard, with bags under his eyes and a rumpled suit. He grips the basin as he stares into his own eyes.*

JIM: Fuck. *(To his reflection)* Nothing to it. Just a date. Regular person thing. I'm just a person going on a date. Just a normal, normal person...
> *Someone leaves a bathroom stall and gives him a weird look. Once alone, Jim continues to talk to himself.*

JIM: Normal person.

CUT TO:

INT. RESTAURANT – EVENING – MOMENTS LATER

> *Maria's face lights up as Jim sits opposite her. She smiles, confident. He smiles back, less so.*

JIM: So sorry. Just got your message.
MARIA: Don't worry.
JIM: Traffic was murder.
MARIA: It's okay.
JIM: It was all backed up, think someone died... Decapitated by their steering wheel or something...
MARIA *(awkward pause)*: Right.
> *Jim shifts nervously, brings a new smile to his face.*

JIM: Anyway, nice to meet you.
MARIA: You too.
> *Maria holds out her hand for him to shake. He takes it.*

MARIA: I've heard so much about you from my sister. She said you're the best programmer she's ever seen.
JIM: Really? She ought to give me a raise then.
MARIA: I'll let her know.
JIM *(hastily)*: Don't tell her I said that.
MARIA: It was a joke.
JIM: Oh.
> *He sighs and closes the menu.*

JIM: Sorry. I'm very rusty.
MARIA: Why's that? If you don't mind me asking.

JIM: Well... I don't know how much Sally's told you about me...
>Maria takes a sip of wine and looks at him seriously.

MARIA: She told me that you keep a wedding ring in your desk drawer along with a photo of a woman with red hair. And that when she told you that I wanted to be set up with you, you looked like she'd just suggested a nice trip to Guantanamo Bay.

JIM: Right. None of that sounds particularly good, does it?

MARIA: To me, it just seems that you're a guy who's been through a shit time, and maybe you deserve a bit of happiness.

JIM *(smiles)*: Yeah. A bit of happiness sounds good.
>They look at their menus.

MARIA: The salad looks good.

JIM: Really? Are you a salad person?

MARIA: Not literally. But yes, I find salad has the best protein-to-carb ratio.

JIM: That's... nice.
>*Jim tried to read his menu but he keeps sneaking glances at Maria.*

JIM: So... why did you want to go out with me?

MARIA: I thought you were handsome and I heard you had a stable career and an almost-six figure income.

JIM: You think I'm handsome?

MARIA: Yes, of course I do. I'm on a date with you, aren't I? What's the point of being here if I don't think you're handsome? I'm assuming you think I'm beautiful?

JIM: Well... yes, but you're very blunt.

MARIA: Yes, I am. I have to tell you, I'm 33 years old and I've been told by my gynaecologist that I only have three more years to have children.

JIM: Ummmmmmmmm...

MARIA: I just thought I should let you know. I'm not messing around here. I just want to find out if you're suitable. You're my third date this week.

JIM: Um?

MARIA: The first one was a surfer. I don't want to end up a single mother.

JIM *(picking up the menu, defiantly)*: I think I'll have the bacon cheeseburger with extra fries. And onion rings.
>*Maria starts to say something, and with the frown on her face it's definitely criticism, but she is interrupted by a LOUD RUMBLE coming from beneath them.*

JIM: What the –
>*Again interrupted by an EVEN LOUDER RUMBLE that causes the ground to shake. Their drinks topple over. The piano music and conversations cut off.*

MARIA: Oh my god!
>*They both get out of their seats, as well as most other people in the restaurant. Everyone is looking alarmed.*

There's SILENCE for a while, long enough for people to relax slightly.

Then – a HIGH PITCHED SHRIEK, ear splitting. Glasses smash and people covers their ears and fall to the ground. Maria falls on top of Jim and rolls off.

EXT. STREET - CONTINUOUS

We see the outside of the restaurant - 'Linguini's', as well as a full high street of shops. The high pitched noise continues as a bright light in the sky appears, getting brighter and brighter and closer to the ground.

INT/EXT. RESTAURANT/STREET - CONTINUOUS

A view of the light getting closer and then landing on the ground, through the window at the front of the restaurant.

As it lands, the noise cuts out jarringly. Maria and Jim struggle to their feet among general panic and make their way towards the window.

MARIA *(awkward)*: Sorry for falling on you...
JIM *(also awkward)*: No problem. Any time.
> *They reach the window and through it they see the light. It starts to dim, slowly revealing what seems to be a huge metal egg on its side. There's no door, no landing gear, just smooth metal and the dimming light.*
> *When the light is off, the outline of a rectangle appears on the side of the egg. The metal inside the rectangle vanishes and a hooded figure jumps the ten feet to the pavement with ease.*

JIM: How...
> *At his voice the figure turns, appears to look straight at him. It raises an arm and beckons to him.*

MARIA *(whispering)*: Is it looking at us?
JIM: It's very hard to tell, isn't it?
MARIA: I think it's looking at us.
JIM: But what if it's not? That'd be embarrassing.
> *He looks behind him to another bystander.*

JIM *(to bystander)*: Is he looking at you? Do you know these guys?
> *The bystander shakes his head. The ground rumbles again. The figure beckons once more.*

MARIA *(shouts over):* Are you looking at us? Shall I like, come over there?
>*The figure nods.*

MARIA: Great. Guess that's happening.
>*They leave the restaurant and walk out into the street, towards the hooded figure, and stand in front of it.*

JIM: Er... hello.
>*Stairs descend from the hole in the egg.*
>*When the figure speaks, its voice is deep and monotone.*

FIGURE: Come.

JIM: Hold on. This seems dangerous. *(Turning to Maria)* I'll make the sacrifice. Take me, not her.

MARIA: Oh come off it. An alien spaceship and an actual alien? You're not taking this from me under the guise of chivalry.

JIM: I'm trying to save your life!

MARIA: Well stop it! I don't need you to protect me, I barely know you. *(Hinting)* I don't even know how old you are...

JIM: Oh, 32.

MARIA: Age 32, with children...

JIM: No children.

MARIA: No children, and good credit... ?

JIM: The best.

MARIA: Okay, that'll do.

FIGURE: Stop that. Get in the ship.

>*Fade out.*

END OF ACT ONE.

Minty Taylor

CRANK

Frustration is a balloon that you don't want to touch the floor, because the floor is made of needles, but your hands are made of jelly, and that just sucks because no one can masturbate with jelly hands. That's a problem for you right now. You've been so caught up with phone calls to phone companies about the meaty mass that is your phone bill, cooking a meal with at least one vegetable, and working out what the hell you just read, that you've neglected your sexuality. It's okay. You make time now. You slip out of your pants and your jelly hands glide down your stomach. Lie back, relax. You've earned this.

Three sharp knocks. Your housemate runs downstairs. She opens the door and you can hear the voice of someone short of breath. Is that Tom? Fuck off Tom. Think about Tom. It helps for a minute but then it feels wrong, like you're fifteen and watching people through a keyhole at a party. You zip up, throw on a jumper and dash to the bathroom. Maybe you can relax in here. You can't hear Tom or Lizzie anymore but there's a cobweb in the corner. You shit in here all the time and it doesn't bother you then. Don't think about shitting when you're trying to orgasm, what is wrong with you? It's not working. Maybe tomorrow you'll get some lube or something.

You get what you focus on, that's what your dad always says. Don't think about your dad, that's pretty grim buddy. He's full of shit anyway.

You're back in your bedroom. Of the options (lube or something) you chose the lube. Maybe it's just a friction thing. This should help. You squeeze some onto your hands – ice cream and jelly – and start to touch yourself. It feels better but there's still no sign of an impending climax. You really go for it now, desperate to be relieved. You're so focused that you don't hear the footsteps getting louder. The bedroom door opens.

When you look up you see Lizzie standing in the doorway. Her mouth is open, her eyes wide, and her lungs appear to have filled themselves with helium. You lock eyes for a moment before you look down and start to manoeuvre the duvet to protect what remains of your dignity.

Keep going, she says.

You look up, hesitating as you push the duvet back, and start to move your hand again. She stands there and watches you. You can hear her breathing, feel her distant body heat. This is working. Tom walks in and starts watching you too. Now you're getting somewhere. Is this fulfilling for you or is it just encouraging to have people's support?

It's not working well enough. You thank Tom and Lizzie for their help.

I think I need more people, you say.

They agree and the three of you catch a bus into town. You masturbate throughout the journey – people watch, they can't stop watching. They follow you to the square in the centre of town. Lie down and carry on there. Crowds gather to watch you. One person wolf whistles, a couple more cheer. They film you on their phones. It's all sweat and lube and moans but it's not enough. You go home to bed but you're back the next day, and everyday this week. The mob increases each time. A young man from a nearby bar asks you to come on stage, says the lighting will be better, says it'll help people see you. The bar reaches maximum capacity within an hour and people crowd around the windows. But you can't do it, you can't get it out. You cry. They applaud.

It's Saturday night and you're on stage again. Last orders are called at the bar and you climb down the steps. A tall man in a brown suit approaches you, says he's from The Guardian and he likes your work. You don't know what he means but you agree to meet him for coffee.

Monday morning and you wank in Costa. The guy from the Guardian arrives and you stand to meet him. He declines your offer of a handshake and sits down. He takes notes on everything you say and writes a piece about you. See your picture in his paper, blurred genitals but face in focus. You masturbate over your own photograph.

Phone ringing. You answer it with your left hand. The BBC want you on the One Show and you go on to masturbate live on national television. One of the presenters, Alex, asks why you do it. You say you don't know, you just can't help it, can't stop until you're done.

Have you tried a finger in the back, asks Matt.

It's been a year since you started and you find yourself now, still unable to orgasm, supporting Ed Sheeran at the O2 Arena in London. The show is sold out. Twenty-thousand people watch and film as tears stream down your face. Fireworks go off during your performance. They cheer for you, chant your name and each syllable brings you closer. But still it's not enough. Your set is over and you leave the stage, dry.

It's the Royal Variety Show tonight. You sweat more than ever and shake at the thought that even the Queen couldn't make you cum. You feel the producers' nervousness weigh down on you like a crucifix. Throughout your performance you stare into the eyes of her majesty, begging for her approval, for her blessing. Members of the audience are leaning their cheeks on their fists. One man in the front row is chatting to the woman next to him. You try that finger in the back.

When you meet her after the show, the Queen's eyes scan upwards, from your genitals, to meet yours. You struggle to breathe. You've heard some people are into that. The silence is broken when Queen Elizabeth the second of Great Britain and Northern Ireland asks if you would like a hand.

That's very kind, your majesty, but I feel I must do this alone, you say.

You whimper as you wank in your new room. Your whole apartment looks like a coffee shop in Shoreditch. Your phone rings but you reject the call. You already know. ITV have published the ratings and your show is a flop. Perhaps you'll be recommissioned by someone else. Channel 5 will broadcast anything.

The phone rings again and it's Tom this time. You remember how he helped you in the early days. It could comfort you to hear from an old friend. You take the call, still masturbating. As you reach for the phone you notice the goosebumps on your arm and so pause for a moment to stroke the skin.

You used to be cool, says Tom.

You hang up the phone and taste the salt water that has run down to your lips.

You plan to go back to your roots, to masturbate in the square again. Maybe you can recapture whatever it is you lost. On the train you message a couple of your journalist friends but no one responds.

This is it, your comeback. People will flock to you. You're so excited you might even cum. You march from the station to the square, stroking yourself like a violinist strokes their bow across their strings. You find your spot, lie down and begin. Scream now and clench your facial muscles. This is what they want, a performance. You've kept your eyes closed but your site stumbles back when you feel a tap on your shoulder. People walk past you, some of them wince at the sight of you, some pay no attention. The only flocking is of a group of pigeons to some discarded chips. A police officer is stood above you.

I'm afraid we're gonna have to move you along, she says.

Disappointment is the end of a cigarette. Rejection is the burning on your lips as you take the last drag. You stub out the butt on an ashtray made of diamonds and lie back on your bed. Still no sign of an orgasm and no one left to praise your technique. Would anyone care if it happened now?

Close your eyes and picture the sea. You drift away from the shore on a raft. Now that raft dissolves into the water. Watch as you drown. Taste the salt that lingers on your tongue.

Francesca Thesen

MELA

SCENE 1

> *Lights up on stage. The audience sees a lone figure, with her arms crossed over her chest as if she is holding a baby. She is black and is dressed in traditional Antiguan dress of a long bright skirt in a tartan fabric, a loose fitting white blouse and a headscarf. It is set anytime after 2005, but it is the director's decision whether to visually specify this. The stage is small and is simplistically dressed with a back wooden wall. Baby pink paint is pealing off the wood and the bleached grey underneath is the overriding colour. It is to resemble the small house 'mother' describes in scene 1.*

MOTHER *(to the audience)*: My baby girl was born in hope, dark and true... I can't look at her any more. The pale sickness of this world has twisted and warped her beyond me, beyond herself. It taught her that she was not right in all her seamless glory. I see her here today, (SHE POINTS AT, AND FIXES HER EYES ON, A 'FIGURE' TO HER LEFT, WHILE HOLDING THE 'BABY' IN HER OTHER ARM) ...she has drowned in it, and carries her self-hate burned across her body, bleach scarred. This is a mother's story to an unforgiven world.

> *A warm glow, which mimics natural light, floods the stage. The song 'pick a bale of cotton', sung by Lonnie Donegan, begins to play in the background and the woman starts to pace across the stage. She sings it to her 'baby'. After one full verse the song fades.*

(Singing, upbeat, as she rocks the 'baby' in her arms): Oh lordy, pick a bale of cotton, oh lordy pick a bale a day, Oh lordy, pick a bale of cotton, oh lordy pick a bale a day. Me and my buddy gunna pick a bale of cotton! Me and my buddy gunna pick a bale a day! *(She comes to a standstill and sings the song slowly, like a lullaby)* Gunna jump down turn around pick a bale of cotton, jump down turn around pick a bale of hay, Oh lordy pick a bale of cotton (TRAILING OFF) Oh Lordy pick a bale a day...

> *Pause, then looks up at the audience.*

My baby came out black, black, black as tar, (pauses as she finds the right words) ...she glitter in the light. I see the heat rising off her like on the road in the morning... *(pause as she discovers the thought, looks at baby)* ...she is the morning, my morning, she shine like the shadows beneath the mango tree. She's the cool before eight and the heat after one. I feel her like a pull when she's in the next room, *(smiles in wonder)* only two rooms, pink-painted and small, but the cord that swings between us feels taught *(Moves her hand to her belly)*. She call me to her, dark eyes, and I feel it in here. *(Pause)* When she came out of my belly *(chuckles at the memory)* like a bloody dark stone, smooth skin slick with me, the darkness of her swirled pearlescent across her forehead *(pause as she remembers)*. I could already feel the silence in her even though she scream... *(laughs then looks down at her arms)* lord did she scream! My dark girl, dark as coals in the fire, embers, she burns, true African black, *(still holding the 'baby' in one arm she lifts her other hand to show the audience)* ...darker than me. I Antigua born, I now seen independence come... but family torn from Congo, and the blood still run dark in my veins, though my skin pale as coffee... Not my baby though... I took her to see Mommy, grandmother, *(fixes her eyes on 'grandmother' to her right and speaks in a rush, smiling with pride)* ...Here she is Mommy, here's the baby girl. Look at her, can you see her burning, can you feel her silence? Look at her eyes Mommy, isn't she like the cool before the rain and the spices on the breeze? *(Pauses and turns to the audience)* I wanted to ask Mommy all these things but Mommy say before I even open my lips *(takes a deep breath)* ...Mommy say 'Lord girl, your baby black like pitch...' *(defensive to the audience)* I know my baby black, my baby black... and perfect like the space in between the stars at night... maybe you only see that space if you look close... *(sadly looks down at the 'baby' in her arms, searching)*.

Blackout.

SCENE 2

Mother stands onstage alone. The lights have dimmed a small amount. She has her right arm extended downwards like she is holding the hand of a small child.

MOTHER: If you're white you're alright; if you're brown stick around; if you're black get back...

She mimes grabbing her daughter and smoothing her hair, checks that

> *she is alright. Mother stands back up and takes her daughter's hand again.*

(Slowly, questioning the audience) If you're white you're alright; if you're brown stick around; if you're black get back... ? *(Shakes her head in disgust, then speaks clearly and with purpose)* Yesterday, I got the bus to the market in St Johns. Took my baby, held her hand the whole time. My baby shy, even though she a big girl now *(smiles)* ...had to do all my groceries one handed, Lord it was hard! Dropped ackees on the floor and me and baby girl just watched them roll, *(laughs)* ...not even for ackees am I letting go of baby girl's hand if baby girl don't want me to! Baby girl gunna be a doctor when she big, but everyone need their Mommy hand until they ready. *(Pauses, suddenly serious)* I saw Shebeeki in the market with her little girl... *(angry)* I see it in their eyes! It is pity! They pity *me*! Why? ... because my baby dark! She dark and beautiful and she blaze if you look close. *(turns to her left still holding her daughter's hand and shouts after 'Shebeeki')* Look at her! *(Drags her daughter with her across the stage as she talks)* Look close and then you will see! *(Pushes her daughter in front of her, as if to show Shebeeki)* She is the cool dark at fifteen-meters down, and she shimmer, jeweled, like the back of a cicada as she sit in the sun. Please just look, *please, please look!* *(Begins to cry and mimes hugging her daughter, speaks through her sobs)* I promise... if you look, you will see... please, please look, she is like dark coals, she is burning...

Blackout.

SCENE 3

> *Mother stands on stage with her arm raised as if she has it linked around the waist of someone slightly smaller than her. The lights have dimmed a small amount, the space is starting to feel more intimate and claustrophobic because of this.*

MOTHER *(chanting):* White, white skin is how you win, all that matters to your kin, if you're black, stay out back... white, white skin is how you win... *(pause as she looks accusingly at the audience)* They sing it in the playground, skipping rope, ball game, they sing it, they push past her in the hall and sing it and even when they not pushing, they think it. It's in the backs of their eyes and the secret space in their wrist when they shake her hand. It glares at her and she can see it now. *(with pride)* Baby girl is big, baby girl a woman now, a new beautiful woman... as dark as the day she left my belly... *(furious anger she struggles to control)* Baby girl doesn't want to be a doctor no more. She taste it now, in the air, and she hate it almost as much as she hate herself. I know it. I can see it in her eyes. She will peal strips off herself, step out of her skin, hang it on the washing line out back and bleach it in the sun. My baby girl wants to bleach. Bleach away the looks, hate... *(with disgust)* pity. Hang it out and let the sun sear away a darkness she feels as taint, a darkness she... *(defeated)* my baby girl wants to bleach...

Blackout.

SCENE 4

Mother stands alone onstage. The lights have dimmed again, it appears to be almost dusk but the woman's features are still easily visible.

MOTHER *(begins to slowly chant)*: Bio Claire, Idole, Neoprosone, Hydroquinone, Immediate Claire, Bio Claire, Idole, Neoprosone, Hydroquinone, Immediate Claire, *(GAINS MOMENTUM)* Bio Claire, Idole, Neoprosone, Hydroquinone, Immediate Claire, Bio Claire, Idole, Neoprosone, Hydroquinone, Immediate Claire! *(Slows back to normal pace)* I know them, they live in my house, they part of my family now. Baby girl sick with it, they flood her head, seep into her skin and make her sick with it. Baby girl puts on her suit in the morning, and tries to find a job through bleach scars. They burn, and steal, and wreck. *(Takes a deep breath and speaks with purpose)* This sickness is not baby girl's even though it radiate from her burning light skin now. This sickness is yours... *(She inclines her head towards different sections of the audience)* ...and yours. It has spun the world into a pale haze and we stand bleached and discolored in our madness... *(Smiles sadly)* all as helpless as I. *(Pause)* In the beginning we start off black, black, black as tar, black as baby girl when she left my belly, and the sickness that lives in hearts, the back of eyes, and the secret space in wrists, is to blame. The illness that shines out of baby girl's skin is yours and mine, even though we can't feel the burning.

Pause.

(Smiles the sad smile of remembering) My baby girl came out black, black, black as tar and perfect like the space in between the stars at night... If only she could have looked close and seen it...

Blackout.

Artemis Tsatsaki

A ROOM IN THE CASTLE

It was one of those classic nights, sleepless and idle, with the dead-beat sounds of the otherworldly creatures lurking out the window and the party music, barely reaching his ears from the ends of the mansion. The bony branches had submerged into a macabre dance, their leaves the dark hair of a maiden against the wind, as if inviting him to join their midnight cult. The mansion stood, majestic and old, towering the tallest trees and in his room, only the light of some candles broke the blackness. His was young and lean, with circles around his grey eyes. Brone was sliding up and down the room, whispering to himself.

'Fascinating thing; how they say that life can scar you. Scar on the face, on the heart, on the body; a whole lifetime to drop salt on that scar. A small grain at a time... So many do, so many do not, so many have and not have. Some past heroic action? Perhaps too much in the past. They would say one hideous action is enough for a hundred good ones, though. Some shameful action then? And every time he looks at his reflection, there it is. Not in the past... Certainly not... The shame is there to follow him every day... It starts to eat him at night though... Yes, at night when the door is closed... And the whole bunch of them is watching, scrutinizing you like some bloody circus freak... It is like an itch crawling up the spine... Like wanting to reach and rip it off so it does not itch any more... Or bite it off with his teeth... I have always wanted a dog...' he concluded with a subtle laugh.

The dancing music gradually became louder. Brone slowly put his ear against the door. He backed up and looked himself in the eyes against the mirror's glass.

'Oddly enough though, I would always get the fleas without the rest... Oh my, they are having quite a party down there. Are they enjoying our hospitality that much or did their households run out of spirits, I wonder?' Brone asked.

'Undoubtedly, the guests seem delighted. No need to mention how keen they always are to visit us. And I am certain it has to do with the exciting parties. Sure enough, their houses are always packed with spirits, or else how would they acquire such exquisite spiritual skills?' Brone answered.

'Of course. What a lovely idea it was to invite them over. It would be rather unfortunate if anyone had to stay at home on such a beautiful night, when theycan join others that did not like their homes as well.' he replied.

'Did we invite them over?'

'Well, they were looking for us. This time or the previous one, I am not sure, but they were.'

'Really? For us?'

'They were asking if we are still here.'

'I seriously doubt it.'

'If anyone is living in this place.'

'If anyone is living in this place? We would have met them, no doubt!'

'I was referring to us.'

'Well, "living somewhere" is similar to "being alive somewhere", correct?'

'Yes, I suppose.'

'There we go!'

'Oh, you're always ready to crack a joke... Do you remember? There were these men once, who would come up here... What would they say to us?'

'I think they told us to avoid showing up a lot to these parties, because "smoke and alcohol fumes make you pale and sickly"?'

'Just pale? Better say anaemic!'

'Anorexic!'

'Bloodless!'

'Washed out!'

'And we were burning up! Who turned the heating up?'

'And then so cold, as if ice had invaded through the walls...'

'Freezing! Especially at nights.'

'Certain corpses were healthier!'

'But, now we are much better!'

'Much better, indeed.'

'We had been sick for ages.'

'Now, we never get sick!'

'Now, we do not even get headaches!'

'So, I suppose that advice worked towards our own good.'

'Of course it did. Did they ever give us unhealthy advice?'

'There is one thing I cannot bring myself to recall, though...'

'And what might that be?'

'When was the last time the sun came up?'

'What are you talking about? The sun has never been up!'

'You are probably right. Nevertheless, I would swear I saw him at some point...'

'On what? Our life?'

'Does it matter? On whatever it is we have.'

Brone stared at his reflection as if he'd been told of the most absurd thing possible. He was momentarily quiet and then let a hysterical laughter fly out his mouth, even though it had not the slightest hint of joy inside it.

'We will always have each other, that's guaranteed.'

'Isn't that a relief! As if we haven't been through enough.'
'Do you remember when was the last time they left?'
'The last time when who left?'
'The guests, of course!'
'They always leave before the morning hours. And then they leave again. Maybe we should welcome them sometime.'
'I agree, but next time.'
'Unquestionably, next time.'
'Always, next time.'
'There has always been a previous time, though.'
'That is why there will always be a next time.'
'I believe it depends. How long have we been in here?'
'For as long as I can remember.'
'I cannot remember any longer than that. So, yes, we are good.'
'Well, the entertaining part about this is that it lasts for inexhaustible amounts of time.'
'And it bears no surprises, whatsoever.'
'And it is so relaxed and easy-going. If only it were not utterly dull...'
'You know, an amusing fact is how death is not actually that eager to take us! It is men that are so eager... to deliver each other...'
'Come on, now you are taking everything too seriously. Will you start being all doom and gloom? I thought we were having a fun conversation here.'
'I don't know if it is fun, but it is probably not what you would call a conversation.'
'I just did! Besides, that is just a technicality.'
'Ok, fine. I am curious about one thing. What is the first thing that you can recollect?'
'You mean the first thing that popped into my head?'
'No, I mean your first memory.'
'Is there a difference?'
'There is a massive difference. For instance, the question that I asked you just came to my mind. But, I do not remember having asked it before.'
'To hell with that. You don't even remember how we started this discussion!'
'Why? Do you?'
'I most certainly do. You asked me what the first thing that I can recollect is. Frankly, I cannot recollect any time when thisconversation was not happening.'
'And since I have the exact same thoughts... So, it seems like time has been trapped in a circle.'
'If it has that means we are not moving forward. It could not possibly cancel the past. Wait a minute. I think we do remember something... They were all gathered around the box, weren't they? Moaning and staring and somewhere even laughing inside their minds. Like spectators at a freak show.

And we couldn't move, we couldn't blink, we couldn't utter a word. It was a nightmare, only we were awake... Well, not exactly. It was not sympathy, you know, what they experienced. It was the worst fear, just like no one is genuinely afraid of heights, until they find themselves dangling from a cliff, with only one hand separating them from us. They want to do the familiar; they want to be the normal. "Keep in line and do your work. That is the secret of our happiness." Isn't that what they always repeated? It offered them a sense of confidence, harmony and a chance of obtaining enough money for a decent hole in the ground... And when they looked at us, they wondered if there was enough time left. And they panicked and run and got hidden. Because they knew it was coming for them, too...'

He stared deep into his eyes. An overbearing graveness had engulfed them. That would not do; he grinned all too widely.

'God, listen to myself monologue. We should have become an actor.'

'And in what kind of plays would we star?'

'Tragedies, of course. We would slip into the bodies of tragic heroes in dead-ends.'

'Or villains, just looking for entertainment.'

'Or star-crossed lovers.'

'Princes, with dilemmas about existence.'

'And all at a reasonable price.'

'Even free of charge. Besides, what is better as a line of work than pretending to be somebody else?'

'True indeed. We would only repeat what someone else thought.'

'We wouldn't have to say any truths.'

'If you think about it, we wouldn't say any lies either.'

'How can that be?'

'Follow me on this one. The truth is the opposite of a lie. The truth is supposed to shed light on lies, otherwise it would merely be called "fact". But, we wouldn't be talking about facts at all, correct?'

'You are right. We would transport our audience into a world of fantasy! The best part is we would never have to look them in the eyes. We wouldn't have to know if they were actually there. They might as well have been a family of mice, just tiptoeing under the floor boards.'

'That would be the dream for more "lively" times, though. Now, I should find a way to pass time here.'

He glided away from the mirror and towards the door. He tried to go through it, but it was impossible. He tried turning the knob, but he just couldn't grasp it. It slipped from his hand.

'And it appears I will have time in abundance to spend... I need to get out,' he whispered, a restrained tremble in his voice.

'They all say that and then they always give me a hard time, though they know that is exactly what I offer...' said the hooded, hunched figure from behind. He did not turn, only took a glimpse with the corner of his eye. Even though he could not see her face – he wasn't certain about the existence of her face – hecould feel her piercing stare on him.

'What are you doing here?' he whispered, without fear in his voice.

'You tell me... I never appear, unless I am called for,' she answered, a little white grin appearing under the hood. She was wearing an impossible amount of clothes, all ragged and worn out, but quite new in a peculiar sense. Her hood concealed her features, but Brone could see long white hair crawling out of it, like serpents.

'Just give me some time...'

'You've had time, or else I would not be here. You know, I always watch you, but people continue to confuse me. Some beg me to arrive, some avoid everything to make sure they elude me and a few are like you. They take their time, but they come to terms eventually. Once, I took a woman who ordered this phrase engraved on her tombstone: "Still, life would be a bore without beer and cigarettes." These little amusements always help pass the time. I am telling you, sometimes time will just not pass. But, I have things that help me. For example, hearing what they have to say before they go. You had plenty.'

'I am still wondering why...' he said to himself or to her, he could not distinguish.

'They always wonder why, it has nothing to do with acceptance. Do you know why they write down the "cause"? Because, I myself am not a cause; more of an outcome, an aftermath... But, they always have to ask why. I have no why. It is my job.'

She raised her eyes – if those things could be called "eyes". She noiselessly crawled from the corner behind his back, slowly lifted her icy, rotting hand and placed it on him. He shivered upon the realisation – it had not gone through him. Brone suffered the weight of granite being rested upon his shoulder. And the room was not there anymore.

Amelia Vale

THE SOUP OF SADNESS

1. There is a soup. We shall call it the Soup of Sadness. The Soup of Sadness is composed entirely of cabbage. Take one cabbage, blend, add salt and water, then serve with a piece of limp bread.
2. There is also a bathhouse. The bathhouse exists in a narrow street of the Chuo Ward in Kobe city. The bathhouse is a front for yakuza-run prostitution. Tonight, a man named Asao is in attendance.
3. Asao is fifty. He has scrub grey hair, satellite ears, and wears a watch. He has hired a room for the evening. A single room for eighteen thousand yen, with company.
4. He sits inside this rented space, naked except for a robe, and clutches a work bag on his lap. The work bag is full of soup. We see him open the bag, take out one flask, and drink.
5. The air around Asao hovers with steam. The bathtub, a brim with water, lies waiting.
6. To Asao, the space smells like massage oil. To Asao, it smells like sweat and money. He continues to drink the soup. He fumbles with one satellite ear. Asao is used to the taste of his meal. To the foul, green sadness. He laps it up.
7. Before long, the company he has paid for arrives. The company is a short woman. She is pretty, with pleasant features, and wears a painted smile on her lips. Hello, Mr. Asao, she says, stepping in through the door. My name is Yasuko.
8. Our protagonist stands to greet this new acquaintance. Our protagonist puts the soup down in a hurry and fastens the belt of his robe. Hello, Miss Yasuko, he says. Good evening. There is a green stain on Asao's lapel. He notices it in the corner of his eye. Can I get you a drink?
9. He pours a bourbon for himself, then another for his visitor. He mixes each drink with two chunks of ice. We see Asao swallow, yanking his lips right back. We see Yasuko snarl with the sting of her gums. Cheers, they say, and the glasses leave wet stains on the countertop. A refill. Another. They drink and they drink, and then they drink some more. That is how they get to know each other.
10. Soon their cheeks are peach-coloured. Soon, they are prepared. Yasuko sits

next to her client. She leans in close, and she kisses him, and, as she has been instructed, she leads him to the bath. This is how the evening has been planned. This is what Asao had paid for. Together, they undo the knot of his robe.

11. Asao is a fat man. He has a belly like an egg, and unkempt hair that grows in pubic loops from groin to chest. He is heaving. When he climbs into the tub, we can see the water rise an inch or two to accommodate his weight, like a buoyant seal plunging into the ocean. Warm, says Asao. Miss Yasuko smiles.
12. It is Asao's first time in a bathhouse. It is Asao's first time having his hair and body washed by a younger woman. He does his best to relax.
13. Miss Yasuko the assistant works well. Miss Yasuko the assistant massages his scalp with expertise and blends the mixtures into his skin. She works on each segment of the body one by one, a technician repairing her subject; firming, cleaning, calming. She is good at her job. She is good with the soap and the cloth.
14. Does that feel nice, Mr. Asao? She whispers. Her breath blows hot on one of his ears. Asao says yes, it does - and the press of your breasts on my shoulders. And the taste of your perfume on my tongue. It all feels wonderful. I don't – I can't –
15. Yasuko works down his body. Yasuko scrapes the moon of his crotch like a coral reef, all pink, and takes the stem of his sex in one hand. She begins to move it back and forth.
16. Small waves form against Asao as she does so. Small moans fill the silence of the air. There is wetness. There is movement. A window is open somewhere in the room, and steam hurries out towards the night.
17. Asao cums. And for a while, there is nothing.
18. Well done, Mr. Asao, Yasuko whispers. Well done sir.
19. Asao lies there like that, collapsed in the tub for a long time until at last, when her client is ready, Yasuko helps him from the bath. She dries him off with a towel, and dresses him once more in a plain robe. We see Asao take a breath. We see him breathe deeply.
20. Would you like some soup? He asks then, gathering his wits.
21. The question is quiet. Its voice is dim. I have plenty, Asao says, moving over to sit on the bed. Enough to share. My dinner, you see. Cabbage. Would you like some?
22. Yasuko is preening. She is glancing at the round clock on the wall, with its brass edge and long black hands. Her painted lips smile and smile, and outside an alley cat screams.
23. I'll try some, she says, cocking her head to the side. Just a little. This was not how her usual appointments played out. This was not what she had been expecting.
24. It's my wife's, says Asao.

25. I see.
26. It's quite revolting.
27. Oh.
28. Together they eat a mouthful each of green cabbage soup. Of the Soup of Sadness in its entirety. Water, salt and vegetable, served on this occasion without a piece of bread.
29. It is quite revolting, Yasuko agrees.
30. Yes, Asao chuckles. It is.

Isabella Winton

YOU'RE A DOCTOR

I would really rather he died. I've been thinking about those words for years, pondering them in my head, pushing them around in my mouth like boiled sweets, unsure if I can commit to the flavour. I would really rather... he died. I stumble over the sentence, the last two words stuck in my mind. I speak it aloud, and I stammer. The stammering doesn't detract from my conviction; it doesn't change the message. I really would prefer it, if he died.

Short term, it would sting. It would be a waste, but at least it would only be his *waste*. None of his madness would spill onto me any more. He pours his insanities, ounce-by-ounce, pound-by-pound, down my throat. I stay in my house. red raw hands that scratch at rashes on my arms – it's just me that's taking the hit. I am sub-human and small. I did *cross the line*, after all. I guess I'll just deal with what comes and carry on, carry on, carry on.

I reach forward and take the box. Fuck strawberries and other red berries. I want chocolate. The security guard has been giving me odd looks, wondering why it's taken me twenty minutes to choose between two brands of granola. I shrug it off and move around the shop. I'm a stone skimming water, sat in the outskirts of my mind, watching the action from a distance. The next dilemma arrives – orange juice, or apple juice? I wonder what will happen. Maybe he'll die in the time it takes me to find out. Not the security guard. I'm not talking about the security guard.

I end up leaving the juice and head home with just my granola and my purse. I've gone outside, I've interacted with other humans, so now I can say everything is good. I have breakfast for tomorrow morning; I'm doing just fine. There are no missed calls on my phone. He hasn't tried to contact me, and he hasn't died. It's a shame about the latter. My luck has never been that good and he's still out there, driving his tank of a car, working himself into an early grave. I imagine that even on his deathbed he'll have that precious Dictaphone in his handand with his last breath, he'll tell his secretary to have the report typed up for next week before pressing the stop button and slithering out of life for good. The thought stops me. I'm already at my front door, keys in hand, staring, staring, staring at the ground. The past five minutes, the streets I've walked, the roads I've crossed don't feature in my memory. Only the words I've been saying gently to myself on repeat, like a shopping list, make any impression.

'I would really rather he-'

I feel something warm press against my legs. I look down. A little ginger cat looks up at me and meows. Describing the noise as a meow is too kind; it sounds more like a tiny yell.

'Oh no,' I say and bend down to pat his head, 'not you too.'

I still want him to die and he will soon. He's a doctor. He knows these things.

*

You don't know exactly how much time you've got left, but you suppose that no one does really. It's certainly not days or weeks, or even months, but you know it's unlikely you'll see another decade.

You're a doctor. You know these things.

Crohns disease is never good, even when caught in the early stages. Yours wasn't caught for thirty years, so you've lost half of your intestines. Your hand falls to your abdomen, feeling the ridge of the scar that runs from your diaphragm to your groin – not good. Prostate cancer isn't great either. Even if it is slow growing and you're pretty sure they removed all of it in the operation last year. You'll know in two years if you're right when they can run the tests. Until then, you've got other things on your mind.

Your current wife, for example, who right now is screaming at you from outside your office, threatening to kill herself. Would you have allowed this to happen years ago, you wonder? You sit in your chair, motionless, staring at your computer screen. You're reading an email from your son, telling you that you deserve better. You know he's right. But in your response, you tell him that wanting you to separate from your wife is not what children should be saying to their father. They don't have your experience or your knowledge. You have to be right. You won't admit anything else.

That is the problem with you. You don't see it when you look at yourself, but your children do. Your son is twenty-six. Your eldest daughter is twenty-three. And your youngest daughter turned twenty-one a couple of months ago. You sent her a card and paid for a small trip, which she suggested. You've done your job. They've all suggested otherwise at points, but you have a reason for everything. You have done everything right, and it's not your fault they can't see that.

Out of all of your children, it is your youngest that is the hardest to figure out. You haven't seen or spoken to her in a while. Just a few days ago, you saw your son, James, and your eldest daughter, Charlotte, to try to defend your wife and mend the fractures you know she's caused... and to ask how to fix what you've broken. You have seen the good in your wife over the years; your children just haven't been around to see it themselves. You tried to explain why she is the way she is, and that she is trying and that she will change, but James and Charlotte don't even consider what you're saying. James speaks.

'Remember what she did to Grace.'

You sit back in your chair. Your wife has moved to a different room to continue her wailing. What she did to Grace, as James put it, was four years ago. You remember what happened but only briefly. You saw Grace packing her bags with Charlotte sat on her bed staring at you, asking,

'Is this actually happening? Dad, are you actually doing this?'

You stood in the doorway and said nothing, holding your hands up.

*

The little cat is still at my ankles, winding round me, pushing his head against my knees. He bites down on my finger, but I don't mind. The shape of his blanched teeth remind me of little traffic cones, and he's trying so hard to be fierce but it isn't working. I enjoy the brief distraction for a couple of minutes and then push my way inside the house.

I sit on the sofa and look at my hands. Sometimes, I can't believe he did it. I question the memory every time it comes into my head, trying to poke holes in the image, but I find no flimsy details or strange recollections. The scene stands alone in my head, crisp and glowing, like a freshly printed photograph. I see it daily, hourly, every minute. It flashes, like a delusion. There was nothing I could do then but watch him standing in the doorway, saying nothing, nothing, nothing. Holding his hands up as if I wasn't his daughter.

*

There was nothing you could do. Your wife would have left you if you hadn't done as she said. Grace would've gone into foster care if your ex-wife hadn't picked her up. It's not like she was going to be homeless. It was wrong, you know that, but you didn't know what to do. You feel like your mind is slowly unravelling, but you don't know how to explain any of it to them. Could they not see how difficult that was for you? They couldn't make you choose between your wife and your daughter. Charlotte said bitterly that you had already chosen.

You stand up. Sitting down for too long is bad for your knees. You remember the osteoporosis developing in your bones and the cataracts in your eyes. The time you have left is likely less than a decade, you remind yourself. For the diagnoses you've picked up, your prognosis isn't that bad. You can do a lot in ten years. You've given patients that prognosis before.

You're a doctor. You know these things.

There's your house in Iceland that you love. It would be wonderful to have your children therefrom Tokyo. You'd like that. You'd love to live in London for half the year, explore all of the museums and the British Library, and then spend the rest of the year out there in the Icelandic wilderness, exploring. You were thinking of extending the summerhouse by three or four rooms so everyone could go and stay out there for Christmas. You've been to Iceland so many times fifteen times if you remember correctly – and you're dying to live there. Some friends you went to St. Bart's Medical with live near the capital anyway. It's been your dream for as long as you can remember.

Oh, and there's the Geology Degree you've been looking at for a while. Your rocks fascinate you. As you've got older, the urge to stray from medicine has grown. You smile briefly, knowing that forty-five years of your life that you've given to medicine is probably enough. You just want to take pictures of the Nordic scenery and wake up to stare at a mountain range in the distance whilst you sip your morning coffee. Maybe you would even listen to the cricket on the radio. Don't you deserve that after everything? Isn't that what you want?

The thing is, you've been getting back into all of your old habits. You send money to your son to help him with his life in London, because you're his father and it's your obligation. Then your wife whispers something. You accuse your son of scrounging. You push them away; your wife draws you closer.

Do you remember two days ago? You let them know how awful it was. James and Charlotte listened and they tried to help you. You know what you can do? You can leave her. You can live somewhere else. Go to Iceland and live out your days there, breathe in the fresh air, walk those mountains you can see resting in the distance.

You don't know how much time you have left.

So don't waste it on her.

But you know you will waste it on her. You don't see anything else. You rise from your chair and leave your study to check on your wife. She's been quiet for a while now, and you hope she's sleeping. There's always a possibility the silence could be something much worse, and the idea puts a spike in your step – a very sharp spike. For a moment, you wonder what Grace is doing. But quickly, she slips your mind.

*

I'm still sat on the sofa, looking at my hands. My watch has stopped and I miss the predictable ticking. I have nothing to focus on when it's not there. I concentrate on my hands, like I always do in times like this. The silhouette of him is always at the front of my memory. It grabs and twists me every time I see it. My hands are blue from the cold, and I hold them up like he did back then, just for a few seconds. Then I lower them and check my phone. My father still hasn't died which is a shame.

I would really rather he got on with it.

Flora Wood
CASSIOPEIA

Can you hear me? Can you hear my voice? It must be muffled. Fighting its way through all these layers, filtering down through material and muscle, skin and sinew to reach you. This baggy woollen jumper, shapeless and smothering and safe. I'm not hiding you. There's nothing they can do now. We're all that matter. You and me. And you are wanted. You are loved. Are you warm enough? It's freezing tonight. Frost is making the world older. The stars are cold and clear and inconceivably beautiful. Do you know, there are more stars in the universe than there are grains of sand on every beach in the world? An impossible number, but the Cosmos makes it possible. It makes the Earth possible, life possible, you possible. It finds order in chaos. Do you think stars are sad or hopeful? Shining on long after they have died, their light still travelling towards us. Fading or immortal? I can never decide. I can see Cassiopeia. The distinctive 'W'. Cassiopeia. Do you like it? Cassie for short. Because you wouldn't just be a star, you'd be a whole constellation. I can't wait to show you. To take your fragile hand in mine, to trace out Ursa Major, to show you how to find the North Star. To anchor you to a sense of direction. It will be time to go back soon. It's getting late. Back to Hannah's tiny flat. You have to jostle with books and clothes and boxes for breathing space. But you can breathe out here. At night there is no clear separation between earth and sky. The darkness stretches out into the depths of the universe. Infinite space. Just five more minutes. Then we'll go. Ancient astrologers believed that our futures could be read in the stars; that these distant lights governed our existence and mapped out the pattern of our lives. Imagine it. To look up and be certain of yourself. I would never have doubted. Never have faltered, even for a second, when they told me to give you up. When they promised me my future, my life. Would you forgive me if I told you I had been tempted? Would you understand if I told you I was angry? That I hated the fact that this was my decision to make? And I had to make it alone? Then I felt you move, and my life wasn't mine anymore. It was yours. Always.

*

Hannah is cooking. The smell of spices wafting towards me as I climb the dingy stairs. Oregano and Paprika. Are you hungry, Cassie? I'm starving. I would feel bad about staying with Hannah – we're a double burden after all, soon to be a permanent package deal – but I know that she likes having us here. Hannah's always been drawn to chaos. Turmoil intrigues her. The jumbled kaleidoscope of emotions and motives, argument and action. It's where the good stories lie. It's all material. Equilibrium isn't exciting. Perhaps that's why I knocked on her door, bedraggled and desperate; she doesn't run from distress, she revels in it. There's a part of her that stays above it all, cool and almost calculating. I remember going to visit her Grandfather in hospital. He had Alzheimer's. It was heart-breaking to see the confusion on his face as Hannah walked towards him. Later, she wrote a poem. It was stunning. So tragically beautiful that we were all in tears. She was the only one who didn't cry. Now sometimes I can feel her watching, waiting in the wings, moulding us into words. Do you mind, Cassie? I worry that one day I'll open a book and find us, unsuspecting, on the page. Your story hasn't even begun yet. You're still made of imagination.

You've got hiccoughs tonight. Lying in bed, I can see the silhouette of my stomach jolting rhythmically. Try taking a deep breath, count to five, then let it go. Did it help? No? Never mind. I can't sleep anyway. I can't seem to get comfortable. I want to run, to hear my feet pounding on the ground and my breath rasping, to feel physically capable. We'll go running together one day. I'll take you to the beach, and you can splash through the surf, test out your legs, feel your body getting stronger. Happy and healthy...

God, what was that? A wave of pain. Deep and insistent. Another. Crashing over me. It can't be yet. You're not due for another two weeks. We're not ready. I'm not – Christ!

'Hannah!'

Hospital.

Bright lights and white. Blinding clinical brilliance. And pain. A sea of it. I'm drowning. Screaming. Fighting. I can't do this... I can't do this...

A cry. It cuts through the pain, the noise, the confusion. It anchors itself in my body. Somewhere deep and primal. It pulls me back. Urgent and indignant and defiant. I see you. The world is soft.

Hello, Cassie.

*

You're sleeping, cradled in the crook of my arm. I could watch you forever. Study every perfect, intricate detail of your face. You're so small. I keep thinking you'll break if I hold you too tightly. But you're stronger than you look. You stir, and your tiny hand tightens around my finger. The echo of an evolutionary impulse. The nails still soft and delicate.

Hannah's fallen asleep in the chair next to my bed. Her face squashed into her palm. A nurse comes bustling over. She holds out her arms, expectant, waiting for me to place you in them.

'She needs a bath. We'll have her back in no time. Have a rest while we're away.'

She takes you. I feel unnervingly empty. The ghost of you still in my arms. They don't know what to do without you in them, as though they had no function before you.

I watch the clock. The hands moving groggily, like they're desperately tired of ticking away the minutes, hours, days. It carries on, the faithful servant of time. Its martyrdom frustrates me. Hannah's eyes flicker open. She looks sleepily at me.

'Where's Cassie?'

'They've taken her.'

'Don't worry. She's in safe hands.'

The nurse comes back, but she gets distracted by a doctor in the doorway. You're a small white bundle in her arms. Why is she still talking? Why isn't she bringing you back to me? The doctor shakes his head slightly and the nurse shrugs. What are they saying, Cassie? They look at me. Their eyes raking up and down. Assessing. Judging. They don't want to give you back. They don't think I can cope. Because I'm young. Because I'm alone. We don't live in a more liberal age. Everyone is just better at hiding their disgust.

The nurse finally brings you to me. I almost snatch you from her. She frowns.

'Careful. Mind her head.'

Ignore her. You're safe with me, Cassie. Shh, don't cry. I'll always protect you – from everyone and everything.

They've sent Hannah home. They're keeping us in overnight. I don't know why. They keep coming to check on us. On you. The nurse is here again.

'You should put her down for a while. Get some sleep.'

'I'm not tired.'

'You look exhausted. She needs you to be rested and healthy.'

The cot seems so far away. All that space between us.

'In a minute.'

She looks unhappy. I don't care. I can sleep when we get home. When I can have you by me, close enough so I can reach out my hand and know you're there. We can have our own perfect corner of the world. Just you and me. We don't need anyone else.

*

This is your home, Cassie. Do you like it? I know it's small, but there's enough room for you. There will always be room for you. Hannah has constructed the cot and put it beside my bed. There's the blanket she bought for you. It's bright and thick. It'll be too heavy for you. It'll smother you. There, it's gone now. You're safe to sleep. I'll be here if you need me. I sink onto the bed. I feel unbearably heavy. Weights on my eyelids...

I wake with a start. There's a shadow looming over you. Its ragged limbs reaching down, its claws snatching you up. I scream and launch myself at it. Hannah's voice.

'Tessa! Calm down – it's me!'

I can see her now. The whites of her eyes glinting in the moonlight.

'What are you doing in here?'

'She was crying. You didn't wake up.'

'Give her to me.'

'It's fine, Tess. She's quiet now. Go back to bed – you need to sleep.'

I can see you wriggling in her arms. She's holding you too tightly. You're uncomfortable.

'I don't want to sleep! I want her back.'

'Okay, okay. I'm sorry.'

I take you from her. Hold you close. But she's still watching you. She can't draw her eyes away. They devour you, claim you, want you. I turn away and shield you with my body. Finally, she leaves. The door clicking shut behind her. I'm sorry, Cassie. I'm so sorry I fell asleep. It won't happen again. I promise.

There are no curtains for the window. The room is cold. Cold air and the cold silver light of dawn. We can't stay here. Not anymore. Not with Hannah. You're her blank page. She can make you into anything she wants. I won't let her use you. She'll tell them I can't cope alone. They'll watch us, waiting for something to go wrong. I wish we had curtains. They'll be able to see through into the room. I bet they're outside already. Don't worry, I won't let them near you. Can you hear that? Footsteps pounding along the street, coming towards the building. Thousands of them. Making the ground shake. Closer and closer and closer...

There's a sharp knock on the door. Hannah is there. I won't let her in, Cassie.

'Tess? I have to go to work. Are you going to be okay?'

'Fine.'

Her footsteps fade. She's gone to tell them. I know it. She's going to bring them back here and they'll take me away. She'll have you then. That's what she wants. I won't let her.

I need to think. What can I do, Cassie? I need to make sure they can't reach you. I drag the wardrobe across the door, barricading us in, blocking the outside world. We'll have to stay here for now. It's the safest place. But the walls are beginning to warp, Cassie. Can you see? They're caving, melting, exposing us. I can't stop them. My hands can't work fast enough to keep them in place. I'm trying... I'm trying...

The door shudders.

'Tess? The midwife is here. You need to let us in.'

I knew it. They've come to take you away. We're trapped, Cassie. I'm sorry. I'm sorry. There's nowhere to run.

'Cassie is crying, Tess. Open the door.'

No! No, I never will. 'You can't take her! You can't have her!'

'I'm not going to take her. I promise. You need help.'

'Liar! She's not just a story – she's real!'

'I know. She's your baby. Yours! No one is going to hurt her. Please, Tessa.'

There's a man's voice now. They're going to break in. No way out, Cassie. Nowhere to go. They can't take you. I won't let them... I won't... I...

The door is being pummelled. It's inching open. They're coming.

The window. The window, Cassie! It's painted shut. My nails tear at the latches. It's not working. I hurl myself at it. The vane cracks. Kicking again and again until the glass shatters. I scoop you up. We've done it, baby girl. They can't follow us this way.

The door crashes open.

'No! Tessa!'

We fall. A shower of stars.

AUTHOR BIOGRAPHIES

CLAUDIA BESANT is in the second year of her English Literature degree and studied Creative Writing as a module. As well as writing, Claudia enjoys reading, rock climbing, learning Japanese and spending time with her family and friends, whose stories always help to inspire her.

AMY BONAR is in her third year of Drama and English Literature. She mainly likes to dabble in all things dramatic and prance about on stage, but has enjoyed trying her hand at writing too! This is her first published piece of writing.

DANIEL BOX is in the third and final year of his English Literature degree, and writes both poetry and prose. He writes about the encroaching apocalypse, student politics, and how coffee and dragons are in fact Queer entities.

MARTHA BOYD is a third year English Literature with Creative Writing student from Leeds. Her muses include Moomins and Bowie. Martha wishes she could write Bowie back to life; instead she murdered her poor friend Jethro in the poem 'Come Home Jethro' which featured in her Bowie-themed poetry dissertation.

FELICITY BROWN is in her third year studying English Literature. She has a keen interest in the performing arts, and, when she isn't writing, can be found acting and generally being inside theatres as much as people will let her.

SOPHIE BUNCE is a second year English Literature with Creative Writing student at UEA. She is an aspiring writer whose family fail to understand why she'd want to be one but encourage her endlessly nonetheless. She writes stories about people she knows, people she doesn't, and people she wants to.

CHLOE CROWTHER is in the first year of her degree in English Literature with Creative Writing. Her writing has appeared in Young Writers' Anthologies, *Wordsmith Magazine*, *Rife Magazine* and UEA's newspaper, *Concrete*. Chloe loves literature and travel, and she has toured America and Canada in search of independent bookshops.

GRACE CURTIS is a second year student of English Literature and Creative Writing. Her work has appeared in publications like *Cuckoo Quarterly* and *The County Climber*, and on stage at Alphabetti Theatre in Newcastle. Her other interests include rock climbing and staring vacantly into the middle distance. She tweets @GracinhaWrites.

ELLA DORMAN-GAJIC is a poet and playwright. Her spoken word show 'Did I Choose These Shoes?' featured at Brighton and Edinburgh Fringe. She is currently Young Writer in Residence for Broken Silence Theatre, who produced her poetry play 'Trust' in London. Her most recent play 'Divided' debuted at UEA.

BASIL EAGLE is a third year English Literature student. He helped to write for a horror zine with his friend Harry Thomas, *Membrane*. An upcoming project is the creative writing magazine, *Third Eye*, which will be published independently. His short stories are inspired by a mixture of interests and fears.

GUS EDGAR is a second year English Literature student and aspiring film journalist. He likes to contrast his depressing short stories with comedy open mics, so if you see a guy ranting on about how to open a mayonnaise jar sexily, that's him.

SAM EDWARDS is in the third year of his English Literature degree. He has previously been published in the UEA student magazine *Octarine*, and his favourite authors are currently Stephen King and Kurt Vonnegut. His extracurricular hobbies include reading in the bath as much as possible and getting razzed with his friends.

ABBEY HANCOCK is in the second year of her English Literature and Creative Writing degree. Her writing has also appeared within the Creative Writing section of *Concrete*. She scribbles all her ideas for short stories in the back of her favourite purple notebook.

ZAID HASSAN is in the second year of his English Literature and Creative Writing degree. His previous writing has been shortlisted for the Wasafiri New Writing Prize and a mild case of impostor syndrome is having him wonder if he's only here to fulfil the diversity quota.

Born in Western Australia, LIAM HEITMANN-RICE is a second year student of English Literature with Creative Writing. As a writer, his principal preoccupation is the recording of life's amusing banalities – to quote his literary hero Christopher Isherwood, 'I was, and still am, endlessly interested in the outward appearance of people.'

JUDITH HOWE is a second year English lit student at UEA, Vice President of the Creative Writing Society and often found roaming the streets of Norwich looking to buy yet another vintage leather jacket she doesn't need.

BECCA JOYCE is a self-proclaimed narcissist, crime writer and big dreamer. She is currently in the third and final year of her English Literature and Creative Writing degree, and her writing has appeared previously in *Electric Read's Young Writer's Anthology 2016*, and *UEA's City of Stories*.

MARI LAVELLE-HILL is a third year Creative Writing student at UEA, living and writing in Norwich. She has previously been published in *HVTN* and *Octarine* magazines and in the anthology *Volta: An Obscurity of Poets*. Mari also reads at various venues around Norwich, including UEA Live and Volta.

SHANNON ELIZABETH LEWIS is a third-year Creative Writing student at the University of East Anglia from Querétaro, Mexico. She writes mainly short stories about odd things happening to people who may or may not deserve it. Her hobbies include writing poetry that she then instantly hides, rock-climbing, and screaming when she thinks about the future

JAIME LOCK is a second year English Literature with Creative Writing student. As part of a collaborative research project on influential Cornish women in history, she wrote the lyrics to the Cornish sea-shanty, 'Jenny Mopas', and has written six short children's plays for Cornwall Theatre School.

As a child, ADAM MARIC-CLEAVER used to eat leaves at the bottom his garden. Now he does the same, but with food and in houses. He dedicates his story to the whiteness surrounding his biography.

LUCY MAY is in her second year of English Literature and Creative Writing. She is President of UEA's Creative Writing Society, and has had her work featured in *Concrete's* supplement, *Venue*. Usually a prose writer, she was inspired to write the work included by her poetry module last Autumn, exploring themes of memory, place and displacement. She is currently working on a short story in the genre of magic-realism.

Critics are calling JONO MCDERMOTT 'the new legal high in Scottish writing', 'as off the wall as Michael Jackson in Vans', 'a 2:1 for balls'. Last seen meditating on a dragon in Malaysia.

ELLIE MEIKLE is in their second year of study on the English Literature degree and their work has also been published in *The North* magazine. Outside of university, Ellie enjoys hiking and political disappointment.

CATHERINE MELLOR is in her third and final year reading English Literature and Creative Writing although, if she had it her way, it would be Creative Writing with (a little bit of) English Literature. She was inspired to write her story while in an Australian hotel with ceiling to floor windows.

MAGDALENA MEZA MITCHER is in her first year of the English Literature with Creative Writing course. Although she prefers to write poetry, Magdalena has enjoyed branching out and experimenting with short stories and scriptwriting. When she isn't cleaning her kitchen to procrastinate writing, Magdalena loves to sing in her band.

TAMAR MOSHKOVITZ is a second year English Lit and Creative Writing student. Her poetry has featured in the collaborative spoken word project Words w/ Friends. When she's not writing, she's jetting back and forth between Norwich and Israel, trying to figure out where home is, and thinking about the critically acclaimed true crime podcast *Serial*. Mostly just thinking about *Serial*, though.

EILISH MULLANE is a Third Year English Literature and Creative Writing student from Suffolk. In her spare time, she subjects her friends to doing read-throughs of her scripts in accents they can't do, and volunteers at the Norwich Theatre Royal.

MATTHEW NIXON is in the second year of his English Literature with Creative Writing degree. He is the News Editor of *Concrete,* UEA's student newspaper. This short story is the first time any of his creative work has been formally published, but his journalism has previously appeared in *The Independent.*

ALYSSA OLLIVIER-TABUKASHVILI is in her final year of English Literature with Creative Writing. Her work has otherwise appeared in *Octarine* and on her online poetry blog. You can see her inspiration from her French-Georgian background, living in London, sitting in coffee shops and studying many languages and cultures.

HENRY OPINA is a second year English Literature and Creative Writing student. He writes mainly poetry but is starting to work on scripts so that the imaginary arguments he wins in the shower are on paper now. He suffers from a crippling fear of writing short bios due to the pretentiousness of the last one he had to write, so as a safeguard he's memorized three things he loves that humanize him: dinosaurs, Oasis, and the episode of Scrubs where Doctor Cox gives rabies to three patients.

CARA OW studies English Literature with Creative Writing. Her relatives secretly question this life choice but it seems to be working out so far – she will soon be published by Math Paper Press in Singapore. Take that, Aunty! Whilst not sassing family, Cara busies herself designing for *Diaspora Diaries*, UEA's first PoC magazine.

GEORGINA PEARSALL is a third year creative writing student and the managing editor of *Octarine* Magazine, and has received such lofty praise as 'bit depressing' and 'I don't really get it but I'm sure it's good'. If required, she can be found crying under a pile of dissertation notes.

JOHNNY RASPIN is in the second year of his English Literature and Creative Writing degree. His writing has previously appeared in the 2017 UEA undergraduate anthology, *Underpass*, and *Volta: An Obscurity of Poets* in 2018. Away from university, Johnny enjoys playing music in his band, The Thinking Men, while simultaneously being the best husband in the world.

ELLIE REEVES is a second year English Literature and Creative Writing student. Her work incorporates many gritty themes prominent in contemporary society. Her poems have appeared in *Concrete*, UEA's student newspaper, and are featured on the digital platform, Vocal. She is currently completing her first individual collection, which will be published in collaboration with Egg Box Publishing.

FIONA SANGSTER is a third year Creative Writing student at UEA. She plans on continuing her creative career with an MA in Scriptwriting. Her entry, *Independence Date*, formed the first few scenes of her dissertation, for which she has to thank her boyfriend Sam for helping her create.

MINTY TAYLOR is a writer, musician and aspiring sock model. He believes that all writing is a form of masturbation and the wankiest phrase he's ever read is 'distribution of personhood'. This is Minty's second time being published in this anthology. His favourite colour is yellow.

FRANCESCA THESEN is in her third year of studying Drama at UEA. She wants to be an actor, director and scriptwriter and is currently writing her dissertation, which is a full sixty-minute play. After graduating she is doing a year at drama school in London before embarking on her acting career.

ARTEMIS TSATSAKI was born in Athens, Greece in 1997. She is a third year student of English Literature with Creative Writing. Her greatest aspiration is to write great novels that will bring the genres of horror and crime together, as well as plays with a similar style. Work of hers was also included in the *City of Stories* UG creative writing anthology by the UEA Publishing Project. When she is not writing, she spends her time training (aka kicking ass) in Taekwondo and watching anime.

AMELIA VALE is a third year undergraduate student. A writer and online journalist, she is the proud owner of an extensive button up shirt collection.

ISABELLA WINTON is a second year English Literature with Creative Writing student. Her favourite genres of fiction include Historical Fantasy, Crime Fiction and Mythology. She is currently working on a novel which explores the issues of still-birth and postpartum psychosis with elements of Nordic mysticism.

FLORA WOOD is nearing the end of her English Literature degree, with one eye focused on life after university and the other firmly fixed on not falling over at graduation. Her life goals include learning to write in the third person and improving her balance.

EDITORS

EDITORS-IN-CHIEF

Tony Allen
Mireia Molina Costa

EDITORIAL TEAM

Beth Bacon
Georgia Brumby
Lucy Caradog
Amelia Court
Chloe Cox
Josephine Dowswell
Sasha Durance
Francesca Giuliani
Cameron Howe
Callum Huthwaite
Becca Joyce
Laura Labanauskaitė
G Mann
C.E. Matthews
Lucy May
Emily Mildren
Farah Mostafa
Electra Nanou
Alice Noon
Alex Paulley
Beth Reeves
Ellie Reeves
Giorgia Rose
Joel Shelley
Melina Spanoudi
Isabel Voice

EGG BOX COMMITTEE

Tony Allen – President
Mireia Molina Costa – Vice-President
Martha Griffiths – Secretary
Lucy Caradog – Health and Safety Officer
Aliyah Rawat – Equality and Diversity Officer
Alex Paulley – First Year Rep
Ellie Reeves – Social Secretary
Amelia Court – Union Council Rep
Cameron Howe – Workshop Co-Ordinator
Farah Mostafa – Treasurer
With special thanks to Eve Mathews

With thanks to Nathan Hamilton, Philip Langeskov and the department for Literature, Drama and Creative Writing at the University of East Anglia.

Thanks to Emily Benton for design advice.